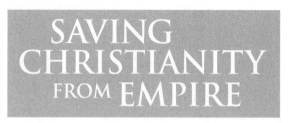

SAVING
CHRISTIANITY
FROM EMPIRE

JACK NELSON-PALLMEYER

SAVING CHRISTIANITY FROM EMPIRE

continuum

New York   London

The Continuum International Publishing Group,15 East 26th Street, New York, NY 10010

The Continuum International Publishing Group Ltd, The Tower Building, 11 York Road, London SE1 7NX

Cover art: Robert Huberman/SuperStock

Cover design: Wesley Hoke

Library of Congress Cataloging-in-Publication Data

Nelson-Pallmeyer, Jack.
  Saving Christianity from empire / Jack Nelson-Pallmeyer.
    p. cm.
  Includes bibliographical references and index.
  ISBN 0-8264-1627-6 (hardcover)
  1. Christianity and politics—United States. 2. Imperialism. 3. United States—Foreign relations. I. Title.
  BR115.P7N365 2005
  261.8'7—dc22
                          2004022015

Printed in the United States of America

05 06 07 08 09 10 10 9 8 7 6 5 4 3 2 1

TO
Sara, Hannah, Audrey, and Naomi

CONTENTS

INTRODUCTION

The words *empire* and *imperialism* enjoy no easy hospitality in the minds and hearts of most contemporary Americans.

—William Appleman Williams[1]

America is a nation with a mission, and that mission comes from our most basic beliefs. We have no desire to dominate, no ambitions of empire. Our aim is a democratic peace—a peace founded upon the dignity and rights of every man and woman. America acts in this cause with friends and allies at our side, yet we understand our special calling: This great republic will lead the cause of freedom.

—President George W. Bush[2]

Our responsibility to history is already clear: to answer these attacks and rid the world of evil.

—President George W. Bush[3]

Feeling like an Outsider

"GOD, GUNS, AND GUTS: THAT'S WHAT'S MADE AMERICA GREAT!" So read giant billboards throughout the Midwest in 1975. This defiant postscript to the United States war in Vietnam was offered by people who had understood the war to be a divinely sanctioned mission in which America's military power sought to spread or protect Christian values

1

and civilization. The intervention went badly. The United States depleted its treasury and lost the war. Millions of Vietnamese were killed along with approximately fifty-eight thousand U.S. soldiers.

The United States, ironically, but not for the first or last time, had destroyed a country it supposedly set out to save and did so with widespread support from Christians. As a college student during the war, I returned to my church one Sunday to preach. In my sermon I said that Jesus' call to love enemies and be peacemakers couldn't be reconciled with U.S. conduct during the war. Many parishioners resented my views and considered me unpatriotic, unchristian, and unwelcome. "Love it or leave it" apparently applied to both church and country. I wasn't ready to abandon Christianity, however, which was and continues to be my spiritual home. Nor was I willing to allow my country to betray principles and harm itself and others without determined protest.

The United States had dropped seven million tons of bombs on Vietnam, more than double the total dropped on Asia and Europe during World War II, and it used poisonous sprays on an area the size of Massachusetts.[4] At My Lai approximately five hundred people, mostly women and children, were ordered into a ditch and methodically shot by American soldiers. The Central Intelligence Agency (CIA) carried out a program of assassination called Operation Phoenix, which, according to historian Howard Zinn, "secretly, without trial, executed at least twenty thousand civilians in South Vietnam who were suspected of being members of the Communist underground."[5] Evidence also surfaced that Washington had manufactured the crisis that justified war. North Vietnamese torpedo boats in the Gulf of Tonkin were said to have engaged in an unprovoked attack on American destroyers. The incident was a fake, and the highest U.S. officials had lied to the public.[6]

The giant billboards trumpeting "God, Guns, and Guts" were deeply disturbing. People who told protestors to love their country or leave it during the war said afterward that they had no interest in exploring the political or faith implications of a disastrous war to which Christians had been complicit. This message—like recent statements from U.S. leaders claiming that God is on our side and that we either support their version of the "war on terror" or are ourselves terrorist sympathizers—made me extremely uncomfortable both as a citizen and as a Christian.

I confess that as a Christian living in the United States I sometimes feel like a political and religious outcast. This has been the case frequently since September 11, 2001. The patriotic sloganeering and music at sporting events, flag lapels gracing the sport coats of TV news anchors, and "United We Stand" and "God Bless America" posters with U.S. flags and Christian crosses—all these didn't and don't speak to my grief, my faith, or my hope for my country. And the militaristic trajectory of U.S. foreign policies as part of the "war on terror," including the war with Iraq and simplistic rhetoric casting U.S. actions in light of the struggle between good and evil, leave me feeling frustrated but determined. The bombs and religious rhetoric that dominated the policies of the George W. Bush administration didn't and don't reflect my hopes and views as a U.S. citizen or as a Christian. I expect more from my country and from my faith tradition. I hope you do too.

Imperial Denial

Language is a powerful conveyer of images, and how we make sense of the world is visible in our most simple formulations. Good versus evil dichotomies did not begin with the administration of George W. Bush. I grew up believing that the United States, a benevolent superpower, was fighting the Soviet Union, an evil empire. The benevolent superpower was strong but good. We sought peace through strength. The evil empire was strong but bad. It wanted to dominate the world and would have succeeded had it not been for our superior military power. "The good news," according to journalist Eric Black's description of the worldview that lies at the heart of our socialization, "was that the United States was even more powerful. We were Number One, and the whole world loved us because all we wanted was peace, prosperity, freedom, and democracy for everyone."[7]

My socialization did not include references to the United States as a benevolent empire and certainly not an evil one. Empire was so strongly associated with a communist menace bent on world domination that in the public mind it became nearly synonymous with evil itself. Most contemporary Americans, therefore, don't associate the United States with empire. That "has not always been the case," however, as historian William Appleman Williams wrote in *Empire as a Way of Life*. "*Empire* was common to the vocabulary of the Americans who made the revolution against Great Britain," including Thomas Jefferson who wrote that "no constitution" was ever before "as well calculated as ours for extensive empire." Williams described how the United States built an empire but in its historical memory turned "the realities of expansion, conquest, and intervention into pious rhetoric about virtue, wealth, and democracy."

Later generations became steadily less candid about these imperial attitudes and practices. They talked ever more about "extending the area of freedom," supporting such noble principles as "territorial and administrative integrity," and "saving the world for democracy"— even as they destroyed the cultures of the First Americans, conquered half of Mexico, and relentlessly expanded the government's power around the globe.[8]

What is most revealing about the January 2004 State of the Union Address quoted above is that the president and his advisors and speech writers used the dreaded word "empire." This means they felt compelled to address the issue of empire in referring to contemporary policies of the United States. "We have no desire to dominate, no ambitions of empire." "America is a nation with a mission," but "our aim is a democratic peace." We have "a special calling" to "lead the cause of freedom." The president's words told us little or nothing about actual U.S. objectives. They revealed much, however, about how people throughout the world saw and *experienced* the United States, including how others made sense of the Bush administration's foreign policies.[9]

The president's denial of empire was born of necessity. At the time of his speech huge numbers of people worldwide, arguably a global majority, believed the United States was an empire or had ambitions to empire, and that its policies were aimed at achieving global domination. They rejected ideas propagated by U.S. leaders that the United States had a unique "mission" and "special calling" that justified unilateralism. Official claims that U.S. foreign policies, including war with Iraq, intended to secure a "democratic peace" or serve "the cause of freedom" were dismissed as self-serving propaganda.

Competing Views

A cursory look at the endnotes in *Saving Christianity from Empire* reveals that recent U.S. foreign policies have brought issues of empire into focus. Numerous writers and think tanks have authored books and policy papers offering a broad range of competing views and perspectives on empire. Advocates for U.S. Empire include many liberals, and critics include progressives and conservatives. Some critics, as I will demonstrate in chapter 1, see U.S. Empire as an unqualified disaster, driven by base motives. Among them are those who believe U.S. Empire is a dangerous aberration traceable to the excesses of President George W. Bush and the neoconservatives.[10] Those who see empire as an anomaly think the damage would be undone if and when a new administration comes to Washington. Others who shared disdain for recent imperial policies believe U.S. Empire has a longer history with deeper roots. They anticipate a difficult and lengthy struggle to rebuild a strong republic as an alternative to destructive empire.[11]

Some writers, including many neoconservatives, have avoided the word *empire* but are strong advocates for U.S. Empire. Included in this group are influential policy makers in the Bush administration, including Richard Perle, who chaired the Defense Policy Board (DPB) until his personal profiteering from the wars he advocated created controversy. He resigned his chair while retaining membership on the DPB. According to Perle and coauthor David Frum, the United States is engaged in a global-wide fight to the death against the forces of evil. The key to victory is unilateral exercise of U.S. military power. They claim, despite the global reach of this war and their commitment to U.S. unilateralism, that "America's vocation is not an imperial vocation. Our vocation is to support justice with power." Their depth of arrogance and breadth of vision are reflected in the book's title, *An End to Evil.*[12]

Irving Kristol, of the ultraconservative American Enterprise Institute, argued in a 1997 article "The Emerging American Imperium" that the United States is an empire by request (although he was careful to distance himself from the word *empire*). "One of these days, the American people are going to awaken to the fact that we have become an imperial nation even though public opinion and all our political traditions are hostile to the idea." The term "American *imperium,*" he observed, was "a more subtle term than *empire.*" It wasn't "overweening ambition on our part that has defined our destiny in this way, nor is it any kind of conspiracy by a foreign policy elite. It happened because the world wanted it to happen [and] needed it to happen."[13]

Other supporters of U.S. Empire use the word but are critical of the Bush administration because they believe it had used the wrong means to build the wrong kind of empire, or that it had taken the United States off the path of its unique form of empire. Michael Ignatieff, for example, argues in favor of "empire lite." "Americans have had an empire since Teddy Roosevelt, yet persist in believing they do not." U.S. Empire, Ignatieff writes, "is not like those of times past, built on colonies and conquest. It is an empire lite, hegemony without colonies, a global sphere of influence without the burden of direct administration and the risks of daily policing."[14]

Ignatieff favors "humanitarian empire." He advocates for "a new imperium [that] is taking shape, in which American military power, European money and humanitarian motive have combined to produce a form of imperial rule for a post imperial age." "As an empire run by Western liberal democracies, chiefly America," he writes, "its moral grace notes are all liberal and democratic. Its purpose is to extend free elections, rule of law, democratic self-government to peoples who have only known fratricide."[15] He criticizes the Bush administration because it had rejected "empire lite" in favor of a more ambitious, unilateral, and unsustainable imperial quest. He cautions that "overwhelming military superiority does not translate into security." "Empires that do not understand the limits of their own capabilities do not survive. Empires that cannot balance pride with prudence do not endure. An endless war on terror," he writes, "tempts the empire to overstretch, and when it overstretches, it becomes vulnerable."[16]

Some conservative critics see U.S. Empire as well intentioned but doomed to fail. Clyde Prestowitz, a former Reagan administration official, chose "*American Unilateralism and the Failure of Good Intentions*" as the subtitle to his book *Rogue Nation*. His is a stinging condemnation of U.S. unilateralism, but he believes that although "we are capable of horrible mistakes," "our intentions are usually honorable."[17] Ignatieff agrees. The United States "is an empire without consciousness of itself as such, constantly shocked that its good intentions arouse resentment abroad."[18]

The politics of empire are complex. Not surprisingly, writers who can't agree on whether or not to use the word don't agree on a common definition of empire. I accept the "if it quacks like a duck" proposition of Clyde Prestowitz. In the view of most Americans, Prestowitz writes, empires "are something Europeans or Chinese or Japanese have, but not Americans. Nevertheless, if it looks, walks, and quacks like a duck, chances are it's a duck." He concedes that "America has few direct colonies or territorial possessions in the classic manner of the Britain and Japan of the past. But empires are also measured by their ability to project power, to compel or entice others to do their bidding, to set and enforce the rules, and to establish social norms. If we look at how the United States stacks up in that regard," he continued, "the unmistakable visage of a duck begins to appear."[19]

Claims, Value Judgments, and Hopes

The title *Saving Christianity from Empire* implies two claims, two value judgments, and two statements of hope. The first claim is that the United States functionally is and has been an empire for a very long time. By empire I mean that on a global scale the United States has and seeks to exercise sufficient power over the political and economic priorities of other nations and the international system as a whole so as to serve the interests of powerful sectors within the United States. This presumption of empire suggests that the excesses of the Bush presidency are real and frightening but best understood in continuity with the past.

My first value judgment is that the pursuit, establishment, and defense of empire have profoundly negative consequences for many U.S. citizens and much of the world. The U.S. Empire is today the leading contributor to global insecurity and violence. Its self-proclaimed benevolence is defied by reckless militarism that results in widespread carnage, increased terror, diminished international law, eroded democracy, and reduced living standards at home and abroad.

My first statement of hope is that there is a positive, realistic alternative to U.S. Empire, what I describe as a republic. The government of a republic is concerned with the well-being of all its citizens in the context of its responsibility to the community of nations of which it is a part. The government that serves empire defines itself by virtue of its superior military power and special mission that put it above international law or the community of nations. It uses kindly rhetoric but pursues domestic and foreign policies aimed at global domination in service to privileged sectors at the expense of many U.S. citizens and other people throughout the world.

Citizens must choose between empire and republic. You can begin to taste the difference between republic and militarized empire if you can imagine a nation known for its windmills, effective local and regional transportation systems, hybrid cars, universal health care system, quality housing and education, diverse agriculture, varied arts and culture, fair tax system, generosity and compassion, support for international law and institutions, low poverty rate, clean air and water, sustainable economy, equity, nonviolent conflict resolution, commitments to peace, and enlightened foreign policies (discussed further in ch. 9).

Long before the rise of the neoconservatives, Michael Parenti warned that "the republic is being bled for the empire's profits, not for [the people's] well-being." Real national security, he wrote, "means secure jobs, safe homes, and a clean environment." The U.S. Empire, "which is paid for by their blood, sweat, and taxes, has little to do with protecting them or people abroad and everything to do with victimizing them in order to feed the power and profits of the few."[20]

The high domestic and international costs of U.S. Empire and the strength of the worldwide revulsion against it may lead to a long-overdue reassessment of the role of the United States in the world. This could lead U.S. citizens to reject empire in favor of republic as part of a nonimperial future. I share a hope similar to that expressed by Paul Krugman: "I have a vision—maybe just a hope—of a great revulsion: a moment in which the American people look at what is happening, realize how their good will and patriotism have been abused, and put a stop to this drive to destroy much of what is best in our country."[21]

The second claim implicit in the title *Saving Christianity from Empire* is that Christianity is distorted because of empire, and that a destructive U.S. Empire is made possible, at least in part, because of distorted Christianity. There is, of course, no single Christianity, no one correct interpretation of the Bible, and no unified Christian support for empire. The Bible presents diverse and irreconcilable images of God, incompatible explanations for historical disasters or triumphs, and conflicting ideas for how to live a faithful life. Christians often search the Bible for meaning and find what they want and need: a loving God; a wrathful God; a wrathful God who loves them; a loving God who hates their enemies. The veritable witches' brew of biblical images, many of them violent, lends itself nicely to politicians determined to defend or expand empire, including a president who has spoken with the assurance of God and viewed U.S. Empire as God's gift to the world.

My second value judgment is that Christians must reject Christian complicity with empire. Mutually reinforcing links between destructive empire and distorted Christianity are deeply troubling and must be challenged and changed. The politics of empire are woven with numerous religious threads. Some are relatively easy to see. These include President Bush's frequent references to God in public pronouncements, speeches peppered with overt or subliminal biblical references,[22] foreign policies described in relation to the nation's special mission, and recurrent use of apocalyptic categories of good versus evil that dangerously oversimplify and distort complex issues. As Benjamin Barber writes, President Bush is "motivated by an overriding belief in the potency of missionary rationales for and military solutions to the challenges of global insecurity." Bush defines "the war for American security . . . in terms of a vision of exceptional American virtue and a countervision of foreign malevolence." This, Barber observes, "may strike outsiders as self-righteous and even Manichaean (dividing the world into camps of the good and the evil) but . . . [it] is powerfully motivating within the United States and . . . gives to his policies an uncompromising militancy invulnerable to world public opinion."[23] Why pay attention to public opinion when you hear the voice of God?

Christianity needs to be saved from empire. It is equally true, however, that the republic, a realistic alternative to empire, must be saved from violent and theocratic streams of Christianity. Legalistic Christians have embraced Bush, a wrathful God, theocracy at home, and militaristic foreign policies abroad. The apocalyptic worldview and messianic pretenses of a president and his supporters among the so-called Christian right, however, are only the most visible threads in the religious web of empire. Christian support for U.S. Empire extends well into mainstream Christianity, where traditional Christians often support destructive U.S. foreign policies and where mainstream Christian theologies allow violent images of God to simmer and take root. As I will demonstrate in chapters 6–7, the Bible and Christianity are dominated by violent images of God and violent story lines that can be reasonably interpreted to justify human violence against others in service to God.[24]

Violent, diverse, and contradictory portraits of God, troubling explanations for historical catastrophes, good-versus-evil dichotomies, and incompatible story lines concerning empire make the Bible a useful and dangerous book in the hands of militarists. It is a particularly dangerous weapon in the hands of President Bush and his followers. As the leader of the most lethal empire in human history, Bush sees himself as God's emissary and believes that U.S. military power is an instrument of God's justice or God's vengeance. Some Americans even think that their military might is an instrument to hasten God's plans for an apocalyptic end time.

U.S. leaders have justified unilateral military action, including preemptive war, because, as President Bush said, "America is a nation with a mission," and it has "a special calling." According to this logic, we are God's new chosen people, on a mission to rid the world of evil. Frum and Perle wrote that "a world at peace, . . . if it ever does come, . . . will be brought into being by American armed might and defended by American might, too."[25] The result of linking violent foreign policies to divine call, as Barber states, is that "self-righteous wrath is steeped in the lore of American exceptionalism. Believing that the United States is unique allows hawkishness to roost in virtue, uses innocence to excuse righteous war, and employs sovereign independence to rationalize strategic unilateralism."[26]

Other troubling threads in the Christian embrace of empire are best seen in light of the larger problem of religion and violence. Religion today contributes to violence, intolerance, and hatred in many ways. It is a dangerous component in many contemporary conflicts where violence against the other is justified in relation to God. "Sacred" texts such as the Bible and the Quran provide inspiration to many people, but they all too frequently inspire to violence. They are dangerous books in the hands of those who claim to know the heart and will of the divine.

Osama bin Laden and George W. Bush are both engaged in holy war. Both have claimed that God is on their side, and both have staked their claim in their respective "sacred" texts. Reflecting the intensity of his faith and using Scripture to justify violence, Osama bin Laden "in compliance with God's order" said, "It is an individual duty for every Muslim" "to kill the Americans and their allies—civilian and military."[27] Reflecting the intensity of his faith and using Scripture to justify violence, President Bush has launched a global crusade against evil. "We've come to know truths that we will never question: evil is real, and it must be opposed," President Bush said.[28] President Bush's policies blend "manifest destiny" and "gunboat diplomacy" with Christian images to create a national ideology of a God-sanctioned crusade against "evils" our nation helped to create. Moral and religious certitude coupled with denial of U.S. complicity allowed Bush to become, in Michael Mann's blunt terminology, "a desk-killer, giving orders resulting in the deaths of thousands from the security of his office."[29]

Martin Marty describes how "scripturally revealed monotheism can serve those minded to be lethal in distinctive ways."

> Believe in one all-powerful God. Believe that this God has enemies. Believe that you are charged to serve the purposes of God against those enemies. Believe that a unique and absolute holy book gives you directions, impulses, and motivations to prosecute war. You have then, the formula for crusades, holy wars, jihads, and, as we relearned in the year just passing, terrorism that knows no boundaries.[30]

My second statement of hope is that Christians can and should embrace a nonviolent, anti-imperial stream of Christianity. Christians living in an empire where patriotism, nationalism, Christianity, and militarism all too often meld together have an obligation to come to terms with violence, including violent foreign policies and violence at the heart of the Bible and the Christian tradition. The idea of "saving Christianity" from empire implies that arguably authentic and less-imperial expressions of Christian faith are possible. Christians must choose between imperial and anti-imperial expressions of Christian faith.

Christianity began as a nonviolent, anti-imperial religious reform movement within Judaism and later morphed into the official, militaristic religion of the very violent Roman Empire. Understanding this historical transformation of faith, from anti-imperial to imperial, nonviolent to violent, can help us come to terms with how and why Christianity became the U.S. Empire's most powerful legitimating engine of imperial pretenses. More specifically, it can help us understand how it is possible that Jesus advocated nonviolence and love of enemies, and yet the United States, where 84 percent of adults identify themselves as Christian, is easily the most militarized country in the history of the world![31]

In the midst of violent story lines that dominate the Bible and most expressions of Christianity, there is a nonviolent, anti-imperial stream associated with the historical Jesus. This nonviolent stream challenges imperial understandings of human and divine power and rejects the notion that superior violence saves. It models creative nonviolence, encourages community, and affirms the nonviolent power of God. As Christians living within U.S. Empire today, we must ask ourselves, "How are we to live given that we grew from an early movement of Jesus followers who were non-violent and anti-imperial?" Our embrace of the nonviolent, anti-imperial stream linked to Jesus could transform Christianity and would allow Christians to become a catalyst in broader efforts to help the nation transition from empire to republic.

This book is written especially for people who are troubled by the arrogance manifested frequently in the policies of the nation and the practices of many Christians. Patriotic sloganeering, flag waving, good-versus-evil rhetoric, and presumptions of divine support for war and U.S. Empire are commonplace. They leave me feeling sad, frustrated, and determined. Both as a citizen and as a Christian, I reject arrogant militarism justified as part of a divinely sanctioned crusade against evil. I have a different vision for my country and for my faith tradition. U.S. Empire undermines our republic, endangers the world, and distorts Christianity. Like the world itself Christianity needs to be saved from empire. And because many

Christians support an empire that undermines our republic, it can also be said that the republic needs to be saved from destructive expressions of Christianity. Imperial Christianity serves empire and not the republic I long for, not the God or Jesus I relate to. It reflects a profound crisis of faith that requires political and religious transformations.

A scene from Denise Giardina's compelling novel about Dietrich Bonhoeffer comes to mind. Speaking to German pastors after Hitler's rise to power, Bonhoeffer urges pastors and the church to take "direct political action" in response to growing persecution of Jews:

> [Bonhoeffer says,] "One course of action might be a pastors' strike. Suppose, in response to the measures taken against the Jews, the pastors of Germany refused to perform their duties. No weddings, no baptisms, no funerals until the anti-Jewish measures are dropped. Consider what a powerful statement to the German people." More pastors leave the audience, some talking angrily as they exit. Dietrich finishes quickly, stumbling a bit over the last of his speech— ". . . a national church which accepts Nazi policies may be popular, but it will never be Christian. The choice before us is clear, Germanism or Christianity"—then steps away from the lectern and nearly runs into the waiting Niemöller. "Have you gone mad?" Niemöller demands. [Bonhoeffer responds,] "Someone must begin to say these things."[32]

We need to speak openly and candidly about the problem of Christian complicity with U.S. Empire. This much-needed discussion depends on an honest assessment of empire; thus in chapters 1–5 I probe the history and present manifestation of U.S. Empire. These chapters make clear that U.S. citizens must choose between empire and republic, and that doing so involves changes that go far beyond sending the neoconservatives out to pasture.

Christians living in the United States also face a stark choice that is not unlike that between "Germanism or Christianity," as posed by Bonhoeffer. We must decide between U.S. Empire and Christianity. This means choosing between violent, imperial Christianity that serves U.S. Empire and a "mustard-seed" variety that embraces a nonviolent, modest alternative rooted in Jesus of Nazareth. Chapters 6–8 explore the religious dimensions of empire. They make clear that alternatives to imperial Christianity require changes far deeper than simply rejecting the most militarized expressions of Christian faith. Chapter 9 describes some of the specific choices we face as Christians and as citizens living in and seeking alternatives to empire.

In his book *American Empire* (1970), John Swomley warned of the dangers of national arrogance rooted in messianic pretenses. His words are shockingly relevant for Christians living in the U.S. Empire today:

> It is precisely when a nation begins to think it is good enough to represent God in chastising other nations that it is in greatest trouble. Its self-righteousness or arrogance of power, as well as its efforts to contain others, breeds antagonism, increases rivalry, and leads to war. A nation that believes it has a messianic role in history, with responsibilities thrust upon it to save civilization by using its power against rival nations, is itself a serious threat to civilization.[33]

Notes

1. William Appleman Williams, *Empire as a Way of Life* (New York: Oxford University Press, 1980), viii (emphasis in original).

2. President Bush, State of the Union Address, January 20, 2004.

3. President Bush, "Remarks at National Day of Prayer and Remembrance," at the National Cathedral, September 14, 2001.

4. Howard Zinn, *A People's History of the United States 1492–Present* (New York: HarperCollins Publishers Inc., 1999), 476.

5. Ibid.

6. Ibid.

7. Eric Black, *Rethinking the Cold War* (Minneapolis: Paradigm, 1988), 9.

8. Williams, *Empire as a Way of Life,* viii–ix (emphasis in original).

9. All references to the Bush administration, unless otherwise stated, are to the administration of George W. Bush and not that of his father.

10. When assessing perspectives on foreign policy, political science identifies several different schools of thought. So-called *political realists* have a rather pessimistic view of human beings, who are understood to be motivated primarily by self-interest, power, and fear. Realists see domestic and international relations as arenas of struggles for power. Realists focus on consequences rather than means or see little or no relationship between foreign policy and personal morality. For realists, the only effective deterrent to aggression is countervailing power, generally understood as military power, to defeat and deter. So-called *political idealists* have a more benign view of human nature. They stress relationships between means, goals, intentions, and outcomes. Political idealists believe that although international conflicts sometimes lead to war, they can often be resolved or avoided through international law and global institutions. States can and often do work together to

resolve differences, and they seek the common good through expansion of trade and working within the United Nations and other international forums. So-called *neoconservatives* have much in common with political realists. Each believes the world is a dangerous place, marked by struggles between states over power; outcomes trump means or morality, and superior military power is needed to defeat and deter aggression. Neoconservatives seem to share political realism's view that human beings are motivated by self-interest, power, and fear—except when they assess their own motives, which are always noble. What distinguishes neoconservatives from traditional conservatives and from some other political realists is their belief that aggressive and often unilateral exercise of U.S. military power can effectively reshape the world in the image of the neoconservatives themselves. Because they emphasize military power as do realists while using rhetoric about democracy and human rights as do idealists, neoconservatives appear as a strange hybrid that cuts across many traditional boundary lines. Their primary goal (see ch. 3), however, is clearly permanent empire through the use and expansion of U.S. military power, and this is why their policies have triggered hostility worldwide.

11. I believe governing an empire is radically different from governing a republic. Government in service to empire seeks global domination in service to elite sectors—energy, military, corporate—whereas government in service to republic is concerned with the well-being of all citizens in the context of a nation's responsible participation in the community of nations.

12. David Frum and Richard Perle, *An End to Evil: How to Win the War on Terror* (New York: Random House, 2003), 279.

13. Irving Kristol, "The Emerging American Imperium," *Wall Street Journal,* August 18, 1997.

14. Michael Ignatieff, *Empire Lite: Nation-building in Bosnia, Kosovo and Afghanistan* (London: Vintage, 2003), 2.

15. Ibid, 20, 112–13.

16. Ibid., 3, 6.

17. Clyde Prestowitz, *Rogue Nation: American Unilateralism and the Failure of Good Intentions* (New York: Basic Books, 2003), 15.

18. Michael Ignatieff, "The Burden," *New York Times Magazine,* January 5, 2003, 24.

19. Prestowitz, *Rogue Nation,* 25–26.

20. Michael Parenti, *Against Empire* (San Francisco: City Light Books, 1995), 69.

21. Paul Krugman, *The Great Unraveling: Losing Our Way in the New Century* (New York: W. W. Norton, 2003), 20.

22. Bruce Lincoln has examined "a vast subtextual iceberg" of biblical images and references in President Bush's speeches. See Bruce Lincoln, *Holy Terrors: Thinking about Religion after September 11* (Chicago: Chicago University Press, 2003), 30.

23. Benjamin R. Barber, *Fear's Empire: War, Terrorism, and Democracy* (New York: W. W. Norton, 2003), 39.

24. This is a problem for many religions, especially including monotheistic religions. For a discussion of how violence dominates the Bible and the Quran see Jack Nelson-Pallmeyer, *Is Religion Killing Us? Violence in the Bible and the Quran* (Harrisburg, PA: Trinity Press International, 2003).

25. Frum and Perle, *An End to Evil,* 279.

26. Barber, *Fear's Empire*, 41.

27. Emergency Net NEWS Service, 1998.

28. State of the Union Address, January 29, 2002.

29. Michael Mann, *Incoherent Empire* (London: Verso, 2003), 4.

30. Martin E. Marty, "Is Religion the Problem?" *Tikkun Magazine,* March/April 2002.

31. See Chalmers Johnson, *The Sorrows of Empire: Militarism, Secrecy, and the End of the Republic* (New York: Metropolitan Books, 2004).

32. Denise Girardina, *Saints and Villains* (New York: Fawcett Books, The Ballantine Publishing Group, 1998), 156–57.

33. John M. Swomley Jr., *American Empire: The Political Ethics of Twentieth-Century Conquest* (New York: Macmillan, 1970), 33.

WILL TO POWER

Because America loves peace America will always work and sacrifice for the expansion of freedom. The advance of freedom is more than an interest we pursue. It is a calling we follow. . . . As a people dedicated to civil rights, we are driven to define the human rights of others. . . . America seeks to expand, not the borders of our country, but the realm of liberty.

—President George W. Bush[1]

If the citizens of the United States were indeed the devoted patriots they call themselves, they would surely not thus encrust themselves in the hard, dry, stubborn persuasion, that they are the first and best of the human race, that nothing is to be learnt, but what they are able to teach, and that nothing is worth having, which they do not possess.

—Englishwoman Frances Trollope in 1825[2]

I fear politicians when they come bearing morality.

—Michael Mann[3]

Mother Teresa with a Gun

Judged by the rhetoric of its architects, an apt metaphor for the Bush administration's foreign policy since 9/11 is Mother Teresa with a gun: global service through smart bombs, torture, daisy-cutters, and cluster bombs. "Our responsibility to history is already clear," President Bush said three days after the World Trade Towers fell, "to answer these attacks and rid the world of evil."[4] Such U.S. rhetoric embodies what Benjamin Barber has called "President Bush's missionary zeal in prosecuting the war on terror—a kind of *High Noon* cowboy righteousness."[5] In a speech at West Point the president said: "Our nation's cause has always been larger than our nation's defense. We fight, as we always fight, for a just peace—a peace that favors liberty."[6]

By the time President Bush cited America's "special calling" in his State of the Union Address in January 2004, the U.S. "mission" didn't resemble a "just peace." Iraq lay in ruins. The fear-generating lies used to justify and gain support for the war had been exposed, and officials reluctantly admitted that no weapons of mass destruction (WMDs) were to be found. Administration efforts to blame "faulty intelligence" for the wide gap between Iraq's nonexistent as opposed to hyped threat had also been discredited. Evidence of U.S. torture of Iraqi and Afghan prisoners by U.S. authorities had been reported, ignored, and temporarily covered up. Thousands of U.S. soldiers and tens of thousands of Iraqis had been killed or wounded, terrorist dangers had escalated, and Afghanistan outside the capital city of Kabul had been largely abandoned to warlords.

This litany of failure tended to obscure from U.S. audiences a core "success" that lay at the heart of these otherwise incomprehensible missions. As Chalmers Johnson wrote, "After the attacks of September 11, 2001, we waged two wars, in Afghanistan and Iraq, and acquired fourteen new bases, in Eastern Europe, Iraq, the Persian Gulf, Pakistan, Afghanistan, Uzbekistan, Kyrgyzstan."[7] As part of the "war on terror," the United States had cozied up to brutal regimes that not coincidentally sat on or near significant oil reserves and offered the United States permanent or semi-permanent military basing rights.[8]

In this context of multiple failures and one hidden success, President Bush reaffirmed "our special calling" and America's "mission" to "lead the cause of freedom." Not surprisingly, his words sounded reasonable and inspiring to many U.S. citizens but fell on deaf ears in much of the world. "The [U.S.] public had been made compliant with imperialism by fear of the alien unknown and an extraordinary self-muzzling mass media," historical sociologist Michael Mann wrote. The United States was losing "the second ideological war [which] is the more important one. This is the one abroad, where the Empire is being established."[9]

In dozens of countries vast majorities rejected the well-cultivated politics of fear and the noble rhetoric that accompanied the U.S. invasion of Iraq and broader "war on terror." As Benjamin Barber wrote in *Fear's Empire,* "American autonomy, American virtue, American democracy, and American innocence—[all] are reasserted with patriotic ardor at home, even as they are deemed hollow and hypocritical abroad."[10] Outside our borders, foes as well as allies considered the United States a self-interested, dangerous bully. Nelson Mandela called the United States a grave threat "to world peace. . . . They think they are the only power in the world. . . . One country wants to bully the world." French historian Emmanuel Todd wrote that in "only a few months" after 9/11, because of arrogant U.S. actions, "the image of a narcissistic, nervous, and aggressive America replaced the images of a wounded nation that was both admired and indispensable for the world's sense of balance."[11]

What seemed obvious to much of the world was unthinkable for most U.S. citizens of empire: *"The United States itself has now become a problem for the rest of the world."* Todd wrote, this America—a "militaristic, agitated, uncertain, anxious country projecting its own disorder around the globe—is hardly the 'indispensable nation' it claims to be and is certainly not what the rest of the world really needs now."[12] Michael Mann warned similarly that the United States had "greatly exaggerated its powers, that it could only found a militaristic Empire, not a benevolent one, and that it will destroy many lives, including American and British ones, before finally undermining the very basis of its own power." In stark contrast to President Bush's claims that the United States is without imperial ambition and has a divinely sanctioned mission to bring democracy and peace to all, the United States is "an incoherent Empire," Mann declared, "whose overconfident, hyperactive militarism will soon destroy it."[13] Benjamin Barber stated, "The paradox is that an America that believes itself so innocent that it must be saved from the rest of the world by assuming a fearful solitude—or transform that world by imposing a fearsome hegemony over it—puts not only that world but itself at grave risk."[14]

Blinders

Defenders of empire seem to share a similar psychological profile that allows them to easily dismiss such criticism. "Like all imperialists," Mann observed, "American ones are self-righteous."[15] David Frum and Richard

Perle, for example, lambasted critics of U.S. unilateralism, including those who opposed the war with Iraq. "The jealousy and resentment that animate the terrorist also affect many of our former cold-war allies." "The same European governments that hesitated to confront terrorists were more than prepared to oppose *us*."[16] "While our enemies plot," they wrote, "our allies dither and carp, and much of our own government remains ominously unready for the fight." They condemned those in Congress "resenting the war's cost and coveting the money for its own domestic spending agendas," the "respected commentators [who] intone about quagmires and overstretch," "journalists [who] deplore Muslim and European anti-Americanism in a way that implies *we* are its cause," critics who "claimed that the Iraq campaign somehow detracted from the overall war against terror," and "gloomsayers" who were "unembarrassable" because they had "been proven wrong when they predicted the United States would sink into a forlorn quagmire in Iraq" and then "reappeared days later to insist that while military victory had been assured from the beginning, the United States was now losing the peace."[17]

In one particularly revealing passage Frum and Perle pointed out all the things they "knew" to be true, all of which were known to be false. "We knew that the UN inspectors had found and destroyed only some of the weapons that Iraq had declared back in 1991. We knew that Iraq almost certainly built additional weapons, weapons components, and weapons materials in the 1990s. . . . And we knew one thing more: We knew that our own best information had consistently underestimated the danger from Iraq."[18] They also knew there were clear links between Osama bin Laden and Saddam Hussein although unearthing them had been difficult because of "the persistent opposition of the CIA [Central Intelligence Agency] and DIA [Defense Intelligence Agency] to any outside investigation of those links."[19]

Frum and Perle and other advocates of empire are shielded from self-reflection and the thorny implications of actual events by the weight of their rhetoric and the apparent strength of their convictions. The United States has a special mission, U.S. military power is the key to establishing a global era of peace, and the threats against us justify any actions we take to defend ourselves. "For us, terrorism remains the great evil of our time, and the war against this evil, our generation's great cause. We do not believe that Americans are fighting this evil to minimize it or to manage it," they wrote. "We believe they are fighting to win—to end this evil before it kills again on a genocidal scale. There is no middle way for Americans: It is victory or holocaust."[20]

Joseph Schumpeter's description of imperial Rome seems apt:

> There was no corner of the known world where some interest was not alleged to be in danger or under actual attack. If the interests were not Roman, they were those of Rome's allies; and if Rome had no allies, then allies would be invented. When it was utterly impossible to contrive such an interest—why, then it was the national honor that had been insulted. The fight was always invested with an aura of legality. Rome was always being attacked by evil-minded neighbors, always fighting for a breathing space. The whole world was pervaded by a host of enemies, and it was manifestly Rome's duty to guard against their indubitably aggressive designs. They were enemies who only waited to fall on the Roman people.[21]

Dangerous Virtue

A nation that inflates the dangers it faces and the mission it assumes as divine mantle is likely to be a threat to self and others. America believes, Barber wrote, that "it possesses unique extralegal prerogatives based on its exceptional righteousness." "The whole point of exceptionalist reasoning is to exempt the United States from universal precepts with respect to war."[22] Claes G. Ryn in *America the Virtuous* describes how benevolent rhetoric often masks powerful ambitions:

> This kind of desire for power rarely shows itself in its own tawdry voraciousness. Those who have it want not only to dominate others but feel good about doing it, even want to have the applause of others for assuming such high responsibility. They feel the need to dress up their striving in appealing garb. Hence the will to power almost always presents itself as benevolent concern for others, as an unselfish wish to improve society or the world. The desire for empire is thus accompanied by a noble-sounding ideology for how to make the world better. So benevolent and comprehensive are its objectives that those charged with carrying them into practice must have virtually unlimited power.[23]

Theologies, ideologies, or mythologies of benevolence are needed and cultivated by advocates of empire whether or not they are believed by those who offer them. Noble intentions mask exploitive policies and serve as emotional cover when believed and ideological cover when not. They are generally more dangerous when believed and internalized, and most dangerous when linked to God and a religious sense of mission. It is hard to know when noble intentions are offered up crassly and consciously to serve imperial objectives and when they are offered sincerely but serve imperial objectives nonetheless. Human beings are capable of both. Consider the words of U.S. Senator Albert J. Beveridge in a speech delivered in 1898:

> God has . . . made us the master organizers of the world to establish system where chaos reigns. He has given us the spirit of progress to overwhelm the forces of reaction throughout the earth. He has made us adept in government that we may administer government among savage and senile peoples. Were it not for such a force as this the world would relapse into barbarism and night. And of all our race He has marked the American people as His chosen nation to finally lead in the regeneration of the world. This is the divine mission of America, and it holds for us all the profit, all the glory, all the happiness possible to man. . . . What shall history say of us? Shall it say that we renounced that holy trust, left the savage to his base condition, the wilderness to the reign of waste, deserted duty, abandoned glory? No! They founded no paralytic government, incapable of the simplest acts of administration. . . . They unfurled no retreating flag. That flag has never paused in its onward march. Who dares halt it now—now, when history's largest events are carrying it forward?[24]

Crass rhetoric or deeply held conviction? It's hard to say. Beveridge himself admitted that the goals of the United States were not primarily altruistic. "American factories are making more than the American people can use. American soil is producing more than they can consume. Fate has written our policy for us; the trade of the world must and shall be ours. . . . We will cover the ocean with our merchant marine. We will build a navy to the measure of our greatness."[25]

Let's consider the same question through the more contemporary lenses of President Bush and Vice President Cheney. Dick Cheney was and is an unusually crass politician who under the cover of 9/11 sought to militarize conflicts and take control of the world's oil supplies in order to benefit himself and his friends in energy and military-related businesses.[26] Cheney received a $26.4 million compensation package in his last year as

CEO of Halliburton. He also held an additional $46 million in Halliburton stock. Halliburton received billions of dollars in "no-bid" contracts in Iraq despite having defrauded the U.S. government on prior contracts on numerous occasions.[27] This corporation was positioned to make as much as $18 billion from its work in Iraq alone.[28] William Hartung, Director of the World Policy Institute, wrote that "Cheney's relationship with Halliburton is a perfect case study of all that is wrong with the relationship between our democratic form of government and the corporations that finance our elections and feed at the government trough on a daily basis." And of "all the loyal, secretive, inside-dealing cronies in the Bush camp, Cheney is the unrivalled master of the game."[29]

President Bush was and is similarly a calculating politician but the more dangerous because he seems to believe, as do many of his born-again Christian supporters, that God chose him to be president. Bush Junior didn't consult his earthly father; he consulted his heavenly Father, and among the things God told him to do was to invade Iraq and Afghanistan. Both Cheney and Bush, in other words, have made the United States, as Todd has argued, "a problem for the rest of the world." President Bush and others who engage in religious pursuit of empire are particularly danger-ous, however, as are their anti-imperial, religious zealot counterparts in al-Qaida. "I've heard a lot of 'God knew something we didn't,'" Ralph Reed, former president of the Christian Coalition, reported. "In the evan-gelical mind, the notion of an omniscient God is central to their theology. He had a knowledge nobody else had: He knew George Bush had the ability to lead in this compelling way."[30]

According to President Bush and many of his supporters, God chose Bush and the United States for a special mission. Marking the first year anniversary of the 9/11 terrorist attacks, the president said:

> I believe there is a reason that history has matched this nation with this time. America strives to be tolerant and just. We respect the faith of Islam, even as we fight those whose actions defile that faith. We fight, not to impose our will, but to defend ourselves and extend the blessings of freedom. We cannot know all that lies ahead. Yet, we do know that God has placed us together in this moment. . . . And the duty we have been given—defending America and our freedom—is also a privilege we share. We're prepared for this jour-ney. And our prayer tonight is that God will see us through, and keep us worthy. Tomorrow is September the 12th. A milestone is

passed, and a mission goes on. Be confident. Our country is strong. And our cause is even larger than our country. Ours is the cause of human dignity; freedom guided by conscience and guarded by peace. This ideal of America is the hope of all mankind.[31]

Our values, Bush declared, "are God-given values. These aren't United States-created values."[32] "The implication was clear," Ryn wrote: "To spread American values was to be on the side of God, to resist them was to oppose God."[33] Ryn perceptively warned that the "human being who thinks himself one of the gods and acts accordingly will bring great suffering on others before he is finally struck down by nemesis."[34] As President Bush himself has vowed, "*We will export death and violence to the four corners of the earth in defense of our great nation.*"[35]

President Bush's faith has seemed to be heartfelt, politically calculating, and dangerous. Doug Thompson in the June 2004 article "Bush's Erratic Behavior Worries White House Aides" wrote:

President George W. Bush's increasingly erratic behavior and wide mood swings has the halls of the West Wing buzzing lately as aides privately express growing concern over their leader's state of mind. In meetings with top aides and administration officials, the President goes from quoting the Bible in one breath to obscene tantrums against the media, Democrats and others that he classifies as "enemies of the state." Worried White House aides paint a portrait of a man on the edge, increasingly wary of those who disagree with him and paranoid of a public that no longer trusts his policies in Iraq or at home. . . . [A] picture of an administration under siege has emerged, led by a man who declares his decisions to be "God's will" and then tells aides to "fuck over" anyone they consider to be an opponent of the administration. "We're at war, there's no doubt about it. What I don't know anymore is just who the enemy might be," says one troubled White House aide. "We seem to spend more time trying to destroy John Kerry than al Qaeda and our enemies list just keeps growing and growing."[36]

Exceptionalism

Arrogance, self-serving myths, and empire did not begin and will not end with the administration of George W. Bush. Citizens living in an influential nation such as ours have an obligation to be engaged, to peel away mythologies of benevolence and imperial theologies of divine mission, and to look at actual policies and practices. We should take to heart Harvard Professor Irving Babbitt's statement in 1924 about U.S. exceptionalism: "We are willing to admit that all other nations are self-seeking, but as for ourselves, we hold that we act only on the most disinterested motives. . . . If the American thus regards himself as an idealist, at the same time that the foreigner looks on him as a dollar-chaser, the explanation may be due partly to the fact that the American judges himself by the way he feels, whereas the foreigner judges him by what he does."[37]

Peel away the rhetoric and at the core of U.S. foreign policy and U.S. Empire one finds a *will to power*. Advocates of U.S. Empire presume that the United States has almost unlimited power. They believe U.S. military superiority is unprecedented and that it can be effectively employed to maintain or expand empire. "At no time in history has the international security order been as conducive to American interests and ideals," the Project for the New American Century declared in a September 2000 report. "The challenge for the coming century is to preserve and enhance this 'American peace.' Yet unless the United States maintains sufficient military strength, this opportunity will be lost."[38] The report said the United States could and must use its unparalleled power to pursue its interests and to guarantee permanent U.S. military superiority that was warranted self-evidently by our goodness. "Preserving the desirable strategic situation in which the United States now finds itself [with no global rival]" "requires a globally preeminent military capability both today and in the future."[39]

The "will to power," Ryn observed, "is most palpable in foreign affairs." What scared much of the world and awakened a growing number of U.S. citizens from political slumber was the fact that many U.S. leaders "seriously contemplate the possibility of ruling the entire world," which they see as a U.S. right "by virtue of its unique commitment to universal principles."[40]

Strength or Weakness?

Many people who have rejected or at least criticized aspects of U.S. Empire have accepted the premise of awesome U.S. power. Benjamin Barber, an articulate and strong critic, for example, admitted that "AMERICAN HEGEMONY IS [*sic*] not in question."[41] "What is compelling" in the arguments of those who advocate aggressive use of military power (he calls them eagles) "is that the unrivaled global dominion of American military, economic, and cultural power means there can be no viable world without America: no prosperity for the poor, no rule of law for nations, no justice for peoples, no peace for humankind."[42] According to Michael Ignatieff, U.S. power is undeniable:

> Yet what word but "empire" describes the awesome thing that America is becoming? It is the only nation that polices the world through five global military commands; maintains more than a million men and women at arms on four continents; deploys carrier battle groups on watch in every ocean; guarantees the survival of countries from Israel to South Korea; drives the wheels of global trade and commerce; and fills the hearts and minds of an entire planet with its dreams and desires.[43]

Other critics, this author included, believe U.S. leaders have grossly inflated the country's benevolence and its real power. They have dramatically overstated the usefulness of U.S. military power to achieve goals such as reducing the threat of terrorism, establishing a compliant government in Iraq, or achieving global domination.

Emmanuel Todd shares this skepticism. He explained that for the United States, as was true for the Soviet Union (whose demise he rightly predicted), the "expansion of military activity" was seen "as a sign of increasing power when in fact it serves to mask a decline."[44] "America no longer has the economic and financial resources to back up its foreign policy objectives." Huge trade deficits with the rest of the world signal that "financially speaking America has become the planet's glorious beggar." It has become the chief "predator of the globalized economy." Its "dramatic militarization" has made it "a superpower that is economically dependent but also politically useless."[45]

Many U.S. citizens have unconsciously internalized values of empire and are unaccustomed to hearing the United States referred to as "planet's glorious beggar," "predator of the global economy," or "politically useless." As novelist and social critic Gore Vidal observed, it is hard for "a nation that sees itself as close to perfection as any human society can come" to heed such criticism. This is especially true because "we are never to be told the truth about anything that our government has done to other people."[46] There are psychological benefits to believing that our nation is number one, benevolent, indispensable, and chosen by God. But high costs too.

When "We" Doesn't Include Us

Michael Parenti included an important *social class dimension* to his criticism of empire in his book *Against Empire* (1995). He stated that empire serves particular interests and groups while undermining the well-being of others. People "must be shown that the republic is being bled for the empire's profits, not for their well-being."[47] According to Parenti:

> Some people reject this critique as "conspiracy theory." They do not believe that policymakers may sometimes be lying and may have unspoken agendas in the service of powerful interests. They insist that, unlike the rest of us, the rich and powerful do not act with deliberate intent. By that view, domestic and foreign policies are little more than a series of innocent happenings having nothing to do with the preservations of wealthy interests. Certainly this is the impression officials want to create.[48]

Without a class analysis of empire, citizens more easily get caught up in patriotic slogans about defense of the nation and the need to support our troops. They also are more easily swayed and victimized by exceptionalist rhetoric that heralds our nation's benevolence and unique mission to the world. The U.S. soldiers killing and dying in Iraq did so not to expand freedom or defend the republic. They served as cannon fodder for U.S. Empire. They killed and died on behalf of elite policy makers whose imperial interests were wrongfully conflated with those of citizens of the republic. One of the remarkable features of U.S. citizen support for U.S. Empire during the Bush administration was how long it took many citizens to see a rather obvious relationship between the energy and military-industrial complex interests of Bush, Cheney, and the neoconservatives, and the militarized foreign policies they pursued under the cover of 9/11. "The push for American empire," Ryn wrote, "is portrayed by its proponents as a great moral cause." "As if by sheer coincidence," he explained, "benevolence has the effect of increasing the power of the allegedly virtuous reformer."[49]

The "U.S. leaders must convince the American people that the immense costs of empire are necessary for their security and survival," Parenti declared. "When Washington says 'our' interests must be protected," however, "we might question whether all of us are represented by the goals pursued." Writing years before the Iraqi debacle drained the U.S. treasury, Parenti (in 1995) warned that "*empire increasingly impoverishes the republic.*

Operational costs of global militarism may become so onerous as to undermine the society that sustains them, such as has been the case with empires in the past."[50]

By this reckoning the U.S. Empire, and even the pursuit of empire, is a disaster. It is neither benevolent nor sustainable. It reflects weakness, not strength. The United States flails about with blunt instruments of destructive militarism. Its perpetual wars show destructive rather than real power, reveal weakness because there is minimal capacity for reconstruction, and hasten the demise of the republic because imperial pursuits threaten U.S. democracy and the well-being of its own people. As Mann stated, "The new American imperialism is becoming the new American militarism. But that is not sufficient for Empire."[51] Benjamin Barber similarly warned that U.S. leaders "pursue a reckless militancy aimed at establishing an American empire of fear more awesome than any the terrorists can conceive. Promising to disarm every adversary," he continued, "to deploy 'the mother of all bombs' and remove the taboo against the tactical use of nuclear weapons, to shock and awe enemies and friends alike into global submission, the beacon of democracy the world once most admired has abruptly become the maker of war the world most fears."[52]

The U.S. Empire is internally and externally destructive. Its mission is exploitation, not freedom, democracy, or benevolence. Among its principal aims is to control oil and other resources. "Since a free and democratic order is slowly being sapped of its substance within the United States," Emmanuel Todd wrote, "the country's goal can hardly be to defend such an order abroad. From now on the fundamental strategic objective of the United States will be political control of the world's resources."[53] The United States, he said, suffers "delusions of empire"[54] and is on a collision course with its own delusions. Policies based on destructive military power serve selective interests, but they show weakness, not strength, and they don't translate into effective control. U.S. "power to constrain militarily and economically is insufficient for maintaining the current levels of exploitation of the planet."[55] According to Todd:

> The limited military, economic, and ideological resources of the United States leave it no other way of affirming its global importance than by mistreating minor powers. There is a hidden logic behind the drunken sailor appearance of American diplomacy. The real America is too weak to take on anyone except military midgets. By provoking all of these secondary players, it can at least affirm

its global role. Being economically dependent on the rest of the world, it will have a global presence of one kind or another. The insufficiency of its real resources is leading to a hysterical dramatization of second-order conflicts.[56]

Empire as Aberration?

The unusually stark imperial trajectory of U.S. policies following September 11, 2001, rightfully alarmed many people. The U.S. Empire, however, did not begin on September 12, 2001, and it will not end when a new administration replaces it. Recent efforts to expand and solidify empire are best understood in continuity with the past (see ch. 5). I close this chapter by citing two writers who expressed relevant concerns about U.S. Empire *decades before* the rise of the neoconservatives.

In *American Empire* (1970) ethicist John M. Swomley Jr. warned that the "actualities of [U.S.] foreign policy are not always as moral as the popular assumptions or the official explanations." "Occasionally some realist will identify the national interest with a more idealistic purpose such as the spread of democracy," he reported. "There is little evidence to support such a hypothesis." U.S. policies revealed "an orientation towards the use of military power as the decisive factor in world politics" designed to maintain a global "status quo." So-called realists, he said, "believe other nations are less just or enlightened," and this justifies "the use of power by their relatively enlightened nation to checkmate the selfish power of other nations."

Swomley, like Parenti (who wrote twenty-five years later), warned that "it is a mistake to think of a nation-state as a unit with a common purpose or a national interest. The machinery of the state," he warned, "is in the hands of one or more groups that use propaganda appeals to patriotism" to "mold a unit consciousness" and thus serve their own interests. "It may be that some men in positions of leadership are aggressive or greedy or attribute to their own nation *a messianic character to save the world from some evil ideology,* but this does not mean that every citizen or even a majority would approve external aggression without the stimulus from and the rationale of the few." He observed that "those who make the decisions about foreign affairs are largely or entirely drawn from certain economic and military elites who find it difficult to separate their own class or group interests from what they call the national interest."[57]

William Appleman Williams also criticized U.S. Empire long before the rise of the George W. Bush administration and the neoconservatives. In

1980 he warned that we had "only just begun our confrontation with our imperial history, our imperial ethic, and our imperial psychology," and he counseled the U.S. people "to define a non-imperial future."[58] Unfortunately, few leaders within the Republican or Democratic parties have shown or show much interest in doing so. As Andrew Bacevich, professor of International Relations, recently stated: "In all of American public life there is hardly a single prominent figure who finds fault with the notion of the United States remaining the world's sole military superpower until the end of time."[59]

The problems of U.S. Empire will not go away with the advent of a new administration. It *is* true, however, that the neoconservatives occupy a rather extreme point on an imperial spectrum and are therefore particularly dangerous. Much of the world recognized this, but many U.S. citizens did not (although increasing numbers do). The front page of the *Washington Post* (Monday, February 24, 2003) described how majorities in many countries throughout the world viewed President Bush as a more serious threat to world peace than Saddam Hussein. As Michael Mann observed, "Americans, insulated within their self-censorship, do not even know how isolated they are in their militarism." "But the world outside is well aware of the contradictions of American Empire. . . . American democratic values are flagrantly contradicted by an imperialism strong on military offense, but weak on the ability to bring order, peace and democracy afterwards."[60]

The world is right in its assessment that imperial ambitions have made the United States a grave threat to people throughout the world, including its own citizens. Its destructive will to power must be exposed and understood so that it can be effectively countered.

Notes

1. Remarks by the president in a commencement address to the U.S. Coast Guard Academy in New London, Connecticut, May 21, 2003.

2. Quoted by Simon Schama, "The Unloved American: Two Centuries of Alienating Europe," *New Yorker,* March 10, 2003; and by Benjamin R. Barber, *Fear's Empire: War, Terrorism, and Democracy* (New York: W.W. Norton, 2003), 63.

3. Michael Mann, *Incoherent Empire* (London: Verso, 2003), 8.

4. President Bush speaking at the National Cathedral in Washington, DC, on September 14, 2001, three days after terrorist attacks destroyed the twin towers of the World Trade Center on 9/11 (Sept. 11, 2001).

5. Barber, *Fear's Empire*, 18.

6. President Bush speaking at West Point Military Academy, New York, on June 1, 2002.

7. Chalmers Johnson, *The Sorrows of Empire: Militarism, Secrecy, and the End of the Republic* (New York: Metropolitan Books, 2004), 214–15.

8. Ibid., 168–85.

9. Mann, *Incoherent Empire*, 104.

10. Barber, *Fear's Empire*, 19.

11. Emmanuel Todd, *After the Empire: The Breakdown of the American Order* (New York: Columbia University Press, 2002), 5.

12. Ibid., 1, xvii (emphasis added).

13. Mann, *Incoherent Empire*, vii, 14.

14. Barber, *Fear's Empire*, 56.

15. Ibid., 100.

16. David Frum and Richard Perle, *An End to Evil: How to Win the War on Terror* (New York: Random House, 2003), 236, 240 (emphasis in original).

17. Ibid., 4, 6, 11, 13 (emphasis in original).

18. Ibid., 23–24.

19. Ibid., 47.

20. Ibid., 9.

21. Quoted in Claes G. Ryn, *America the Virtuous* (New Brunswick, NJ: Transaction, 2003), 196.

22. Ibid., 99–100.

23. Ibid., 4.

24. John M. Blum et al., *The National Experience: A History of the United States* (New York: Harcourt Brace Jovanovich, 1963), 533.

25. Ibid.

26. For former Secretary of the Treasury Paul O'Neill's unflattering portrait of Cheney, see Ron Suskind, *The Price of Loyalty: George W. Bush, the White House, and the Education of Paul O'Neill* (New York: Simon & Schuster, 2004).

27. William D. Hartung, *How Much Are You Making on the War, Daddy?* (New York: Nation Books, 2003), 33, 39–40.

28. William Hartung, "Outsourcing Blame," posted on www.TomPaine.com, May 21, 2004.

29. Hartung, *How Much Are You Making on the War, Daddy?* 26–28.

30. Quoted in Kevin Phillips, *American Dynasty: Aristocracy, Fortune, and the Politics of Deceit in the House of Bush* (New York: Viking, 2004), 224.

31. President Bush's Remarks to the Nation, September 11, 2002.

32. Bob Woodward, quoted in the *Washington Post*, November 19, 2002, cited in Ryn, *America the Virtuous*, 7.

33. Ryn, *America the Virtuous*, 7.

34. Ibid., 3.

35. Ibid., 7 (emphasis added).

36. Doug Thompson, "Bush's Erratic Behavior Worries White House Aides," *Capitol Hill Blue*, June 4, 2004 (www.capitalhillblue.com).

37. Ryn, *America the Virtuous,* 129.

38. "Rebuilding America's Defenses: Strategy, Forces and Resources for a New Century," A Report of the Project for the New American Century, September 2000, iv.

39. Ibid., i.

40. Ryn, *America the Virtuous,* 3–4.

41. Barber, *Fear's Empire,* 19; see also 79 (capitalized words in original).

42. Ibid., 46.

43. Michael Ignatieff, "The Burden," *New York Times Magazine,* January 5, 2003, 22.

44. Todd, *After the Empire,* xvi.

45. Ibid., xxi, 16, 21.

46. Gore Vidal, *Perpetual War for Perpetual Peace: How We Got to Be So Hated* (New York: Thunder's Mouth Press/Nation's Books, 2002), x, ix.

47. Michael Parenti, *Against Empire* (San Francisco: City Light Books, 1995), 69.

48. Ibid., 155.

49. Ibid., 5, 11.

50. Ibid., 46, 62 (emphasis added).

51. Mann, *Incoherent Empire,* 14.

52. Barber, *Fear's Empire,* 15.

53. Todd, *After the Empire,* 20.

54. Ibid., 98.

55. Ibid., 77.

56. Ibid., 132.

57. John M. Swomley Jr., *American Empire: The Political Ethics of Twentieth-Century Conquest* (New York: Macmillan, 1970), 2, 6, 16–17 (emphasis added).

58. William Appleman Williams, *Empire as a Way of Life* (New York: Oxford University Press, 1980), xi.

59. Quoted in Johnson, *Sorrows of Empire,* 67.

60. Mann, *Incoherent Empire,* 120, 261.

UNDER THE COVER
OF TERROR

We had to create a false rationale for going in [to Iraq] to get public support. The books were cooked, in my mind. The intelligence was not there. I testified before the Senate Foreign Relations Committee one month before the war, and Senator Lugar asked me: "General Zinni, do you feel the threat from Saddam Hussein is imminent?" I said: "No, not at all. It was not an imminent threat. Not even close. Not grave, gathering, imminent, serious, severe, mildly upsetting, none of those."

—General Anthony Zinni, USMC (retired)[1]

Why, of course the people don't want war. Why should some poor slob on a farm want to risk his life in a war when the best he can get out of it is to come back to his farm in one piece? Naturally, the common people don't want war, neither in Russia, nor England, nor for that matter, Germany. That is understood, but after all it is the leaders of the country who determine the policy and it is always a simple matter to drag the people along, whether it is a democracy, or fascist dictatorship, or a parliament, or a communist dictatorship. Voice or no voice, the people can always be brought to the bidding of the leaders. That is easy. All you have to do is tell them they are being attacked, and denounce the peacemakers for lack of patriotism and exposing the country to danger. It works the same in any country.

—Herman Goering (Nazi Reichmarshall, Hitler's heir apparent)[2]

At present the United States faces no global rival. *America's grand strategy* should aim to preserve and extend this advantageous position as far into the future as possible.

—The Project for the New American Century[3]

Fearful Agendas

Blinded by patriotism, fear, and those who propagate it for political gain, U.S. citizens became unwitting allies in a reckless pursuit of militarized empire masquerading as a war against terror. Officials in the Bush administration exploited 9/11 in order to implement a previously determined agenda they described as "America's grand strategy." The grand strategy set out to establish permanent U.S. global supremacy through the unilateral exercise of military power.[4] It had little to do with fighting terrorism and in fact was counterproductive to efforts to do so. "Most Americans did not see action against terrorists and their supporters as part of a design for global control," Claes G. Ryn wrote, "but those who did took full advantage of the opportunity to commit the United States to a comprehensive plan for empire."[5] The Bush administration, in Goering-like fashion, inflated threats of terror, questioned the patriotism of critics, and cultivated a politics of fear in service to its broader agenda that could only be pursued through aggressive war on a global scale.

Following the terrorist attacks of 9/11, citizens were led to believe that the world was a dangerous place and that unilateral U.S. initiatives, including unrestrained use of military power, would make us safe, defeat terrorism, and bring democracy and freedom to the world. The threat of terrorism presented the American people with a choice, David Frum and Richard Perle warned: "victory or holocaust."[6] Vice President Dick Cheney jump-started a long public campaign of lies and deception to justify war with Iraq on August 26, 2002: "Simply stated, there is no doubt that Saddam Hussein now has weapons of mass destruction. There is no doubt he is amassing them to use against our friends, against our allies, and against us." Less than two months later Secretary of Defense Donald Rumsfeld warned that Iraq in "a week, or a month," could provide al-Qaida with "weapons of mass destruction" that could potentially kill a hundred thousand people.[7]

Cheney, Rumsfeld, and others who made similar claims were not only mistaken; they were also lying. They exaggerated threats with *full knowledge at the time they made them* that Iraq had neither weapons of mass destruction nor ties to international terrorists such as al-Qaida. As Anthony Zinni, former commander of the United States Central Command (CENTCOM), explained, "We had to create a false rationale for going to war," and so the "books were cooked." "No one in the region felt threatened by Saddam," and his military "didn't have the capabilities that were pumped up, that were supposedly possessed by this military." Zinni said, "The rationale that we faced an imminent threat, or a serious threat, was ridiculous."[8]

A nonpartisan report, "Iraq on the Record," was produced by the United States House of Representatives Committee on Government Reform on March 16, 2004. It documented "237 specific misleading statements" made by President George W. Bush, Vice President Dick Cheney, Defense Secretary Donald Rumsfeld, Secretary of State Colin Powell, and National Security Advisor Condoleezza Rice to justify war with Iraq. A simple definition of a misstatement is a lie. However, for "purposes of the data base," the report stipulated, "a statement is considered 'misleading' if it conflicted with *what intelligence officials knew at the time* or involved the selective use of intelligence or the failure to include essential qualifiers or caveats." The misleading statements by the five notables named above, the report said, reflected "*a pattern of consistent misrepresentation.*"[9]

Administration officials and their supporters served up lies, misleading statements, and misrepresentations. They did so because 9/11 offered them an opportunity to cultivate and capitalize on a politics of fear that would enable them to pursue *previously determined objectives.* These objectives (discussed in ch. 3 as part of a detailed analysis of what U.S. policy makers called "America's grand strategy") included, but were not limited to, establishing permanent control over the world's oil supplies, increasing military spending, militarizing space, establishing new permanent military bases in areas of strategic importance, implementing and showcasing the doctrine of preventive war, developing a new generation of nuclear weapons, and removing multilateral constraints on U.S. power.

Fear-based politics were orchestrated and largely successful within the United States. The majority of the world's people and a minority of U.S. citizens, however, saw U.S. foreign policies, including those pursued under the banner of the war against terror, as grave threats to world peace. Citizens socialized deeply into the myth of the benevolent superpower and steeped in American exceptionalism were unprepared for such criticism. Clyde Prestowitz, a former official in the Reagan administration, wrote:

America can be like a "rogue wave," a large swell that, running contrary to the general direction of the waves, takes sailors by surprise and causes unexpected destruction. . . . While we think of ourselves as the "good guys," we are blinded to our own sometimes irritating behavior by the strength of our mythology and the dominance of our culture. I fear a dangerous gulf is widening between America and its friends as we Americans listen to but don't hear, and look but don't see, the concerns of other countries and at the same time also fail to recognize how some of our behavior flouts our own values. Right now we are attributing criticism of American policies to envy of our success and power and to chronic anti-Americanism. . . . Perhaps we should also look at how we deal with some key issues and how our behavior is perceived and comports with our values.[10]

Unilateralism with a Purpose

Exceptionalism lends itself easily to unilateralism. The architects of militaristic foreign policies, Barber wrote, "are fixed on the sovereign right of an independent United States and of its 'chosen people' to defend itself where, when, and how it chooses against enemies it alone has the right to identify and define."[11] The United States is virtuous, and this entitles it "to rule the world for its benefit. According to this ideology, the United States is no ordinary nation. It is based on universal principles," Claes G. Ryn explained, "the principles of all mankind, and has a higher responsibility and mission than all other countries." "This vision amounts to a new myth of America: the United States as the ruler of a virtuous empire."[12]

Empires act unilaterally because they believe they have the power and the right to set the rules and exempt themselves from the rules they set. The strength of our mythologies makes it hard for us to see this, to receive criticism, or to understand the wisdom of those who see unilateralist U.S. policies as part of an imperial project. To pursue its "grand strategy," the United States needed to remove multilateral constraints that restricted its power. This meant a frontal assault on the international system, including undermining various international institutions and agreements. Unilateralist sentiments were widespread in both the Clinton and Bush (George W.) administrations. Clinton's Secretary of State Madeline Albright defended U.S. unilateral military action thus: "If we have to use force it is because we are America! We are the indispensable nation."[13] President Bush said that the "course of this nation does not depend on the decisions of others."[14] Earlier he told the General Assembly that the "United Nations must do what we say or it risks becoming irrelevant."[15] Bush also claimed divine mandate: "Our nation is chosen by God and commissioned by history to be a model for the world."[16]

Richard Perle wrote in an article for *The Guardian*, "Thank God for the death of the UN: Its abject failure gave us only anarchy. The world needs order." Perle announced that "Saddam Hussein's reign of terror is about to end. He will go quickly, but not alone: in a parting irony, he will take the UN down with him."[17] Perle along with coauthor David Frum described U.S. unilateralism as undoing "the exaggerated multilateral conceit of the Clinton administration."[18] National Security Advisor Condoleezza Rice expressed similar sentiments when she criticized Democrats for subordinating U.S. interests to "the interests of an illusionary international community" and for believing "that the support of many states—or even better, of institutions like the United Nations—is essential to the legitimate exercise of power."[19]

Clinton's commitment to multilateralism was exaggerated by his critics in the Bush administration. The Center for International Policy (CIP) cohosted a conference in May 1999 with the Royal Institute of International Affairs "to discuss the pros and cons of what many see as a disturbing trend toward unilateralism in U.S. foreign policy." The "Center for International Policy remains firm in its conviction," according to Wayne S. Smith, "that the United States is squandering the best opportunity the world has yet seen to construct an international system based on the rule of law." He observed that the "years of the Clinton presidency have seen the United States drift toward unilateralism and the *undermining of the international system.*"

Smith and the CIP identified a number of disturbing signs of unilateralism: "The U.S. Senate's defeat of the crucially important Nuclear Test Ban Treaty" in October 1999; U.S. refusal "to ratify key international conventions," including the International Convention of the Rights of the Child and the convention banning antipersonnel landmines; "unilateral sanctions against countries with which we disagree"; refusal "to pay arrears to the United Nations"; and U.S. efforts "to limit inspection safeguards in the Chemical Weapons Convention—and lagging in tightening the rules against biological weapons." It appeared, Smith wrote, that Congress's prevailing view holds "that as the United States has emerged as the only remaining superpower, it need no longer adhere to international law."[20]

The Clinton administration also engaged in frequent use of unauthorized military force, thereby setting the stage for the dramatic escalation in military adventurism that characterized the Bush administration. The 2000 Democratic platform called for a new doctrine of "forward engagement" that, according to Congressman Norman Dicks of Washington, would "mean addressing problems early in their development before they become crises . . . and having the forces and resources to deal with threats as soon after their emergence as possible."[21] Clinton ordered bombing raids in Afghanistan, Iraq, and the Sudan without international approval and in clear violation of the UN Charter. In the case of the Sudan, the U.S. bombed a pharmaceutical plant that it mistakenly identified as a chemical weapons plant. It also, along with Great Britain, maintained a punitive sanctions regime against Iraq that violated UN mandates and resulted in the deaths of hundreds of thousands of Iraqi children.

The Bush administration took a series of actions prior to and especially following 9/11 that *continued and accelerated* this pattern of U.S. unilateralism. One of George W. Bush's first acts as president was to issue an executive order cutting off U.S. funds to the United Nations Population Program. This was ostensibly a payback to the religious right, who blamed the UN program for promoting abortions. It had the unfortunate consequence of substantially increasing the number of abortions worldwide because, due to inadequate funding, millions of women lacked access to other family planning options. It also signaled that U.S. hostility toward the United Nations would escalate rather than abate, and it established an early sign of the administration's modus operandi in which unilateral action and rule by presidential fiat were the norm.

Even a partial list of unilateral actions taken by the United States during the Clinton and Bush years is breathtaking in the scope of its arrogance and imperial design:[22]

- Withdrew from the UN population program (Bush).
- Refused to ratify the Kyoto Protocol to reduce global warming (signed by the U.S. in November 1998, rejected by Bush in March 2001).
- Refused to ratify the Convention on Biological Diversity (signed by Clinton in 1993 but never ratified by Congress).
- Refused to sign the Convention on the Prohibition of Land Mines (Clinton and Bush).

- Refused to support international efforts to curb Illicit Trade in Small Arms and Light Weapons (Bush).

- Undermined the Chemical Weapons Convention by conditioning its signature on crippling exemptions approved by the Congress in 1997 that excluded the United States from most of its provisions.

- Refused to ratify a protocol to strengthen the Biological Weapons Convention of 1972. The United States in 2001 was the only nation among the 144 parties to the Convention that rejected the protocol (Bush).

- Rejected the International Criminal Court. The ICC was set up to investigate and prosecute individuals accused of crimes against humanity, genocide, or crimes of war. The United States pressured other nations not to sign onto the ICC and/or to guarantee the United States permanent immunity from prosecution (Bush).

- Undermined the Biological and Toxins Weapons Convention (BWC) by resisting a legally binding enforcement mechanism and by seeking to rewrite the convention to allow the United States to develop and deploy prohibited weapons (Bush).

- Opposed the protocol to strengthen the 1987 Convention Against Torture out of fear that it would interfere with interrogation techniques employed at the prison at Guantanamo Bay and elsewhere (Bush). These interrogation techniques became the subject of great controversy, and feigned innocence, after prison abuses in Iraq and Afghanistan became public.

- Refused to ratify the UN Convention on the Elimination of all forms of Discrimination against Women—CEDAW (signed by President Carter but never ratified), and International Convention on the Rights of the Child (never ratified).

- Refused to ratify the Comprehensive Test Ban Treaty that bans all explosive nuclear tests (rejected by Congress in 1999, also opposed by Bush).

- Abrogated the 1992 Anti-Ballistic Missile Treaty (ABM) on December 13, 2001, that restricted deployment of antimissile defense systems (Bush).

- Announced deployment of a National Missile Defense (NMD) system (developed under Clinton, supported by Congress, dramatically accelerated by Bush).

These unilateral actions, coupled with the invasion of Iraq and a militarized approach to the "war on terror," including the invasion of Afghanistan, undermined benevolent mythologies and made little or no sense in terms of stated objectives. They didn't lessen the threat of terror, expand democracy or freedom, or secure peace and prosperity. They were the actions of a rogue state in conflict with U.S. mythology and accountable to no one. These actions were logical, however, if understood in light of "America's grand strategy" and the unstated imperial objectives mentioned above, including controlling oil, militarizing space, removing multilateral constraints on the exercise of U.S. power, and paving the way for the new doctrine of preventive war ("preemption").

Danger Inflation

The politics of fear prevented most citizens from seeing clearly the reasons for and implications of these unilateralist actions, the militarized war against terror, and the invasion and occupation of Iraq. Emmanuel Todd stated that the United States following 9/11 involved itself in "conflicts that represent little or no military risk [in order] to allow the United States to be 'present' throughout the world. The United States works to maintain the illusory fiction of the world as a dangerous place in need of America's protection." "The exaggeration of the Iraqi threat," he said, "will be remembered as only the first act in America's dramatic staging of nonexistent global dangers that the United States will rush to save us from." This folly would, he foresaw, inevitably "provoke a radical weakening of its position in the world in the near future."[23]

In our grief and in the context of the political theater of fear-mongering, many citizens seemed unable to place the admittedly vicious, deadly, and serious attacks of 9/11 in a reasonable context. Despite 9/11 and the rhetoric of our leaders, the world was not a particularly dangerous place for Americans, although U.S. policies were making it far more dangerous than it needed to be. "Fear is terrorism's tool and catalyst," Benjamin Barber wrote, "the multiplier and amplifier of actual terrorist events that on the global scale are few and far between and, while devastating to those directly affected, are of less statistical consequence than say a year's traffic fatalities or the mundane tragedies of people falling off ladders at home."[24]

The near-apocalyptic interpretation given to 9/11 inflated our sense of danger, which in turn allowed U.S. leaders to carry out dangerous policies in pursuit of empire. Michael Mann wrote in 2003 that "al-Qaeda is actually rather weak," and that before the dysfunctional war against terror began in earnest, "Radical Islamists" had "lost ground" throughout the Middle East. Unfortunately, Mann observed, "cultivating fear is a Bush the Younger specialty." Although Mann acknowledged terrorism as a serious problem, he argued that it would be relatively "easy" to defeat present terrorists and "to stem the flow of future terrorists." Unfortunately, however, "the Pentagon is ingenious . . . in creating more terrorists." "Present international terrorists are being killed, but future ones are being created at a faster rate. What a disastrous war!"

Policies that purported to defend our allies and us and to defeat terrorism in fact made U.S. citizens and the world less rather than more secure. Bombs were blunt, ineffective, and often counterproductive instruments for fighting terrorism. Reducing threats of terror often depend on intelligence and law enforcement efforts, extradition and trial, not daisy-cutters and B-52s. Militarism was a poor substitute for effective policies, but it was embraced by a citizenry crippled by fear and satisfied with revenge. Important differences between national and international terrorists were ignored even though understanding these differences was vital to efforts to reduce terror. Mann said the United States should aim to "separate international terrorists from any nationalist support base," but its policies were having the opposite effect, which could "make life extremely unpleasant for Americans for many years to come." "US policy, if sufficiently stupid," Mann warned, "might end one thousand years of Muslim disunity. It is exactly what bin Laden is kneeling towards Mecca and praying for."[25]

A predictable consequence of fighting a "war against terror" that includes objectives other than fighting terror is increased threats of terror. This absurdity is more pronounced because, as Mann pointed out, "the world is not actually very dangerous."

> It should not be dangerous at all for Americans—so prosperous, so comfortable and so well-protected in the sea-girded continent we dominate. Dangers loom *because* of American militarism—seeking to drive into the ground the few failing communist remnants in the world, seeking extra-territorial control over oil supplies, stationing American troops where they have no business, invading foreign countries uninvited and supporting state terrorists. No significant danger would occur if the US stopped doing all these things. Quite the contrary.[26]

If the United States were seriously interested in reducing terror, it could take a number of rather simple but important steps. For starters, Mann proposed, it could "leave alone conflicts involving national liberation fighters" and "stay away from the quagmires" of failed states. It could "steer clear" of "class or land wars" in places like Colombia, Bolivia, Venezuela, and the "peripheral regions of Indonesia." It could "denounce terrorism and state terrorism equally, and accompany this with its best conciliation services, backed by material incentives for those willing to compromise." It could stop supporting state terrorists and help resolve the Israeli-Palestinian conflict.[27] It could also desist from policies that encourage national terrorists to develop links to and sympathy for international terrorists who have little to offer them and with whom they have little in common:

> [Al-Qaeda doesn't] offer policies which could unite these disparate movements. . . . Al-Qaeda and its allies offer zero prospects of social and economic development for Muslims. All they offer is anti-Americanism. But the more Americans denounce and attack other Middle Eastern governments and movements as part of a single, undifferentiated war on terrorism, the more likely these are to link up with each other and with al-Qaeda. This is the perfect way to convert national into international terrorists.[28]

Our Goodness, Their Pathologies

There were and are literally hundreds of things the United States *could do and stop doing* that would significantly lessen the threat of terrorism. Critics of the Bush administration, therefore, argued persuasively and rightly that U.S. leaders had almost completely botched the "war on terror." Former Vice President Al Gore, for example, said:

> There was then, there is now and there would have been regardless of what Bush did, a threat of terrorism that we would have to deal with. But instead of making it better, he has made it infinitely worse. We are less safe because of his policies. He has created more anger and righteous indignation against us as Americans than any leader of our country in the 228 years of our existence as a nation—because of his attitude of contempt for any person, institution or nation who disagrees with him.[29]

This assessment of dangerous incompetence, while true in itself, can miss two vital problems rooted in empire. First, the "war on terror" is being conducted as part of a grand strategy for empire. Second, international terrorism itself is a consequence of empire. Reducing terrorism is an achievable goal *if your real priority is to reduce terror and if your imperial policies don't generate despair and inflame terrorists.* The inevitable result of pursuing imperial objectives under the cover of a "war against terror," however, is escalating hatred of the United States and increased insecurity, violence, and threats of terror. The "new imperialism," Mann wrote, "creates more, not fewer, terrorists," and it "creates more determined 'rogue states.'"[30]

On September 11, 2001, President Bush told the nation that "America was targeted for attack because we're the brightest beacon for freedom and opportunity in the world."[31] On another occasion he spoke of the war on terrorism as a "crusade" and added in private: "They hate Christianity. They hate Judaism. They hate everything that is not them."[32] Similarly, the president told cadets at the Air Force Academy graduation in June 2004 that the "terrorists who attacked our country on September the 11th, 2001, were not protesting our policies. They were protesting our existence."[33] Even if the president expressed these sentiments sincerely, they are most certainly wrong and dangerous.

Osama bin Laden's motives for attacking the United States were reasonably transparent. As Mann explained, "Bin Laden did not fall from the sky. He was created by the foreign policies of the Soviet Union and then the United States." His grievances are *political,* and his "motives are simple: he is an anti-imperial Islamist." Bin Laden resents "imperialists brutally seizing land and property by force of arms." "There is a simple *reason* he attacked the US: American imperialism. As long as America seeks to control the Middle East, he and people like him will be its enemy." "He attacked American military imperialism. So if the new imperialism takes wing, there will probably be more bin Ladens."[34]

The idea that people reject or attack us because of our goodness, our values, our religion, or our modernity *shifts attention from our behavior, particularly U.S. foreign policies, onto their presumed pathologies.* As Mann observed, it "is a simplistic, ethnocentric way of dismissing any grievances caused by our aggression. . . . They do not hate our culture or our democracy or our wealth, simply our foreign policy."[35] The U.S. citizens have the perception that although people throughout the world didn't support war with Iraq, they did support U.S. military efforts in Afghanistan. Poll after poll in country after country outside the Muslim world, however, showed that overwhelming majorities "favored extradition and trial" rather than war. The "Muslim world was quite hostile," Mann reported. "Bin Laden had declared that the US sided with repressive Muslim regimes, killed Iraqis, stationed troops on holy Muslim soil, and supported Israel against the Palestinians. All these allegations," Mann maintained, "were widely believed, *because they were true.*"[36] That is why, as John Esposito writes in *Unholy War: Terror in the Name of Islam,* many of bin Laden's criticisms of the United States and the West resonate with the "perceptions and grievances of mainstream as well as extremist Muslims."[37]

Shifting the focus from us to them prevents us from probing the causes of anti-American sentiment that sometimes spill over into terrorism. It also all but guarantees that U.S. responses will involve self-righteous and destructive militarism.

> The preferred American story is that their own history, backwardness, poverty and cultural resentment causes terrorism—so that we do not even have to listen to what they say are their actual grievances. Of course, the consequences of this misperception are appalling. Obviously, unlike our present foreign policy, we cannot possibly abandon our overall culture, democracy or wealth. All we can do, if we think these are the sources of their hatred, is to repress and kill them.[38]

At the National Cathedral (Washington, DC) a few days after the terrorist attacks of 9/11, President Bush said: "We are here in the middle hour of our grief. But our responsibility to history is already clear: to answer these attacks and rid the world of evil." The congregation then stood and sang "The Battle Hymn of the Republic." Bob Woodward wrote that the president "was casting his mission and that of the country in the grand vision of God's master plan."[39] According to Woodward, when CIA Director George Tenet reported that going after countries that harbored terrorists would mean war with sixty countries, the president replied: "We'll pick them off one at a time."[40]

Incompetence and Empire

There are terrible outcomes linked to the "war on terror," including endless war, erosion of civil liberties, destructive violence, blood and carnage, depleted budgets, international hostility, increased threats of terror, and violations of human rights. Amnesty International (AI) Report 2004 said that the "'war on terror' and the war in Iraq has encouraged a new wave of human rights abuse and diverted attention from old ones." "While governments have been obsessed with the threat of weapons of mass destruction in Iraq," Irene Khan, secretary general of AI, observed, "they have allowed the real weapons of mass destruction—injustice and impunity, poverty, discrimination and racism, the uncontrolled trade in small arms, violence against women and abuse of children—to go unaddressed." The AI report condemned the "callous, cruel and criminal attacks of armed groups such as al Qa'ida" and acknowledged that these groups "pose a very real threat to the security of people everywhere." "But it is also frightening," Khan said, "that the principles of international law and the tools of multilateral action which could protect us from these attacks are being undermined, marginalized or destroyed by powerful governments." She warned that governments "are losing their moral compass, sacrificing the global values of human rights in a blind pursuit of security. This failure of leadership is a dangerous concession to armed groups."

> The global security agenda promoted by the US Administration is bankrupt of vision and bereft of principle. Violating rights at home, turning a blind eye to abuses abroad and using pre-emptive military force where and when it chooses has damaged justice and freedom, and made the world a more dangerous place.[41]

Certain U.S. policies contribute to horrific outcomes that are made possible by national arrogance, mythologies of benevolence, and the gross incompetence of its leaders. These outcomes, however, must also be understood as *consequences of empire*. Some U.S. leaders may have internalized mythologies of benevolence or deceived themselves that militarism fulfills a divine mission, but they also, as reported above, lied and consciously cultivated and exploited fear-based politics. They assaulted citizens with well-crafted images of pending disaster, including images of mushroom clouds. "America must not ignore the threat gathering against us," President Bush warned. "Facing clear evidence of peril, we cannot wait for the final proof—the smoking gun—that could come in the form of a mushroom cloud."[42]

This and other similar statements were made by administration officials *who knew Iraq wasn't a threat*. Vice President Dick Cheney was desperate to invade Iraq and so frustrated with the volume of intelligence that confirmed Iraq wasn't a threat that he created his own "Office of Special Plans" to cook the books on intelligence. That office manufactured a threat that served as a fig leaf for the invasion of Iraq for reasons having little or nothing to do with stated objectives. General Anthony Zinni also said that "the Defense Department created its own boutique intelligence agency to vet them."[43] Similarly, twenty-seven-year CIA veteran Ray McGovern stated, on the day CIA director George Tenet announced his resignation, that Tenet had corrupted "the Intelligence process to the policy that had already been decided." "He played that game, and he defended it, and if you look at what [the CIA Intelligence] estimate said, it was wrong on virtually every count."[44]

In addition to knowledge that Iraq wasn't a threat, Bush administration officials knew something else that was equally important but left unsaid even by most critics of empire and the war with Iraq. *They knew that the invasion and occupation of Iraq would increase rather than decrease terrorist threats.* As Rahul Mahajan wrote:

> The "war on terrorism" is not a war on terrorism. From the very beginning, there were good reasons to believe that a militaristic response of the kind we have seen since 9/11 would not work and might well, in fact, exacerbate the threat. If the safety of ordinary Americans was a significant concern for the Bush administration, its policies would be very different.[45]

The Bush administration considered *increased terrorism an acceptable cost* within their cost-benefit analysis. Controlling Iraqi oil, establishing permanent U.S. military bases in Iraq, and modeling and establishing precedent for their new doctrine of "preemptive" war—these were the unstated, not-for-public-view, imperial objectives of the invasion. These were instrumental components in a grand strategy aimed at global domination, and their benefits were thought to outweigh the risks or costs of increased terror. As Gore said in his talk at New York University, "A policy based on domination of the rest of the world not only creates enemies for the United States and creates recruits for Al Qaeda, it also undermines the international cooperation that is essential to defeating the efforts of terrorists who wish harm and intimidate Americans."[46]

I'm not privy to the cost they anticipated or how much terror fell within their definition of acceptable outcomes. Iraq proved to be a quagmire, not a cakewalk, a human and financial drain of monumental proportions (they said the costs of the invasion and occupation would come from Iraqi oil revenues), and a terrorist recruiter's dream. The Bush administration tried to cook the books and claim that its policies had resulted in 45 percent reduction in terrorist incidents since 2001, but amid growing scandal it had to retract its rosy portrait.[47] According to a report from a London-based think tank, the International Institute for Strategic Studies, the al-Qaida network "has been galvanized by the war in Iraq [which] focused the energies and resources of al-Qaeda, while diluting those of the global counter-terrorism coalition."[48]

The costs of the Bush administration's folly and faulty cost-benefit analysis may be incalculable. Hopefully, in addition to squandered lives, wasted resources, and increased threats of terror, they will include the administration's downfall and the death of the neoconservatives' specific plans for a militarily imposed permanent empire rooted in "America's grand strategy."

Notes

1. Remarks at the Center for Defense Information Board of Directors Dinner, May 12, 2004.

2. Statement made while imprisoned at Nuremberg after World War II.

3. "Rebuilding America's Defenses: Strategy, Forces and Resources for a New Century," A Report of The Project for the New American Century, September 2000, I (emphasis added).

4. David Ray Griffin, *The New Pearl Harbor: Disturbing Questions about the Bush Administration and 9/11* (Northhampton, MA: Olive Branch, 2004). This well-respected theologian from Claremont School of Theology argues that it wasn't just the *negligence* of the Bush administration that allowed the terrorist attacks, but also its *complicity*. Conspiracies are hard to prove, however, and so I focus on verifiable claims related to the politics of fear. In the next chapter I describe the "grand strategy" pursued under cover of the politics of fear.

5. Claes G. Ryn, *America the Virtuous* (New Brunswick, NJ: Transaction, 2003), 7.

6. David Frum and Richard Perle, *An End to Evil: How to Win the War on Terror* (New York: Random House, 2003), 9.

7. "Iraq on the Record: The Bush Administration's Public Statements on Iraq," prepared for Representative Henry A. Waxman by the United States House of Representatives Committee on Government Reform—Minority Staff Special Investigations Division, March 16, 2004, 7. Available at www.reform.house.gov/min.

8. Remarks at the Center for Defense Information Board of Directors Dinner, May 12, 2004.

9. Ibid., i, 1–2 (emphasis added).

10. Clyde Prestowitz, *Rogue Nation: American Unilateralism and the Failure of Good Intentions* (New York: Basic Books, 2003), 6.

11. Benjamin R. Barber, *Fear's Empire: War, Terrorism, and Democracy* (New York: W. W. Norton, 2003), 37.

12. Ryn, *America the Virtuous*, 8.

13. Quoted in Colman McCarthy, *I'd Rather Teach Peace* (Maryknoll, NY: Orbis Books, 2002), 71.

14. George W. Bush, State of the Union Address, January 28, 2003.

15. George W. Bush, Address to the General Assembly at the UN, September 12, 2002.

16. McCarthy, *I'd Rather Teach Peace*, 71.

17. Richard Perle, "Thank God for the Death of the UN," *The Guardian*, March 21, 2003. www.guardian.co.uk/comment/story/0,3604,918764,00.html.

18. Frum and Perle, *An End to Evil*, 6.

19. Quoted in John Feffer, ed., *Power Trip: U.S. Unilateralism and Global Strategy after September 11* (New York: Seven Stories, 2003), 229.

20. Wayne S. Smith, "The Trend Toward Unilateralism in U.S. Foreign Policy," Center for International Policy, http://ciponline.org/oldiprunil.htm (emphasis added).

21. Ibid.

22. For a description of unilateral actions taken, see Prestowitz, *Rogue Nation*, and Feffer, *Power Trip*.

23. Emmanuel Todd, *After the Empire: The Breakdown of the American Order* (New York: Columbia University Press, 2002), 133–34.

24. Barber, *Fear's Empire's*, 31.

25. Michael Mann, *Incoherent Empire* (London: Verso, 2003), 186–89, 149, 160, 190.

26. Ibid., 266 (emphasis in original).

27. Ibid., 187–88. U.S. citizens are aware that terrorists are often nonstate actors who express their grievances by engaging in terrorism. Mann refers to state terrorism to denote terrorist acts contributed by nations at the behest of their governments. This means a willingness to criticize terrorist actions by states such as Israel as well as those of the United States and other allies.

28. Ibid., 178.

29. "Remarks by Al Gore," as prepared, New York University, May 26, 2004, http://www.moveonpac.com/goreremarks052604.html.

30. Ibid., 15.

31. "Statement by the President in His Address to the Nation," September 11, 2001.

32. Mann, *Incoherent Empire*, 164.

33. President Bush Remarks at the United States Air Force Academy Graduation Ceremony, United States Air Force Academy, June 2, 2004.

34. Mann, *Incoherent Empire*, 169 (emphasis in original).

35. Ibid., 162.

36. Ibid., 125 (emphasis added).

37. John L. Esposito, *Unholy War: Terror in the Name of Islam* (New York: Oxford University Press, 2002), 22.

38. Ibid., 162.

39. Bob Woodward, *Bush at War* (New York: Simon & Schuster, 2002), 67.

40. Ibid, 33.

41. Amnesty International Press Release, "Report 2004: War on Global Values—Attacks by Armed Groups and Governments Fuel Mistrust, Fear and Division," 26 May 2004, http://news.amnest.org/library/print/engpol100162004.

42. Quoted for Waxman in "Iraq on the Record," 9.

43. Anthony Zinni, Remarks at the Center for Defense Information Board of Directors Dinner, May 12, 2004.

44. Ray McGovern, in an interview with Jeremy Scahill on "Democracy Now," www.democracynow.org/article.pl?sid=04/06/03/1626202.

45. Rahul Mahajan, *Full Spectrum Dominance: U.S. Power in Iraq and Beyond* (New York: Seven Stories, 2003), 32.

46. "Remarks by Al Gore."

47. See "Defeating Terror? Not according to 2003 Statistics," the lead editorial in the *Minneapolis Star Tribune,* June 15, 2004.

48. See Tom Regan, "New Reports Question War on Terror," March 28, 2004, csmonitor.com.

3

PLANS FOR EMPIRE

It is time to reaffirm the essential role of American military strength. We must build and maintain our defense beyond challenge.

—*The National Security Strategy of the United States of America* (September 2002)[1]

Even a global *Pax Americana* will not preserve itself.

—The Project for the New American Century

Ultimately, it will be necessary to confront . . . [and] to question the desirability of the United States relying on military force to control the world's oil supply and to suppress all foreign challenges to American domination.

—Michael Klare[2]

"Grand Strategy"

The terrorist attacks of September 11, 2001, provided the Bush administration with an opportunity to implement a previously determined "American grand strategy" for permanent empire. Elements of a "grand strategy" aimed at global empire through unilateral use of military power first surfaced in a 1992 Defense Planning Guidance (DPG) draft. The two notables behind the document were Paul Wolfowitz and Dick Cheney. Wolfowitz, author of the original DPG draft, was at the time Under Secretary of Defense for Policy for then Secretary of Defense Dick Cheney.

During the administration of George W. Bush, Wolfowitz became Deputy Secretary of Defense under Donald Rumsfeld. Wolfowitz and Rumsfeld were leading advocates for preventive war, including war with Iraq, as was Vice President Dick Cheney. The DPG draft circulated within the Defense Department. It laid out guidelines for reshaping U.S. foreign policy in a world in which *U.S. power was no longer constrained* by the defunct Soviet Union.

The DPG draft contained three central themes. "Our first objective is to prevent the re-emergence of a new rival," the DPG draft stated. "This is a dominant consideration underlying the new regional defense strategy and requires that we endeavor to prevent any hostile power from dominating a region whose resources would, under consolidated control, be sufficient to generate global power." The world, in other words, had one superpower, and no other nation or group of nations need apply. No rival would be tolerated anywhere, not in "Western Europe, East Asia, the territory of the former Soviet Union, [or] Southwest Asia." As the world's lone military superpower, the United States was in a unique and advantageous position, the DPG draft argued. The United States should use its dominant position, including its overwhelming military power, to establish permanent supremacy. The "first objective" of U.S. foreign policy, according to the DPG draft, was to capitalize on its strategic advantage in order to "maintain the mechanisms for deterring potential competitors from even aspiring to a larger regional or global role."

A second theme in the DPG draft was that because no nation or group of nations was in a position to stop the United States, its foreign policy should aggressively promote U.S. interests and so-called American values. The United States should use its dominant position and unstoppable military power to "spread democratic forms of government and open economic systems," and to counter regional threats, including threats from countries such as Iraq and North Korea. According to the DPG draft, U.S. military power was unprecedented in scope and without serious challenge. Its effective use would allow the United States to address a variety of problems, such as "access to vital raw materials, primarily Persian Gulf oil; proliferation of weapons of mass destruction and ballistic missiles; threats to U.S. citizens from terrorism or regional or local conflict; and threats to U.S. society from narcotics trafficking."

A third theme in the DPG draft was unilateralism. To turn present military advantages into permanent global supremacy and to use supremacy

chaotic world / order / suppression
for power

as a basis for achieving tactical objectives, the United States needed to act alone. The DPG draft made no mention of taking collective action through the United Nations. It stated that although coalitions "hold considerable promise for promoting collective action," the United States "should expect future coalitions to be ad hoc assemblies" to deal with particular crises. It "should be postured to act independently when collective action cannot be orchestrated."[3]

When leaked to the press, the DPG draft was considered extreme. Defense Secretary Dick Cheney was forced to rewrite it and soften some of its edges. The official Defense Planning Guidance, however, still argued "that the United States should be prepared to use force if necessary to prevent the spread of nuclear weapons . . . (and should) maintain United States military primacy and discourage the emergence of a rival superpower."[4]

Blueprint for Preeminence

The core ideas of Cheney's DPG and Wolfowitz's earlier draft continued to evolve within think tanks such as The Project for the New American Century (PNAC). Established in 1997, PNAC's "Statement of Principles" said that as "the 20th century draws to a close, the United States stands as the world's most preeminent power." But it faces a critical question: "Does the United States have the resolve to shape a new century favorable to American principles and interests?" The United States needed "a military that is strong and ready to meet both present and future challenges." "If we shirk our responsibilities, we invite challenges to our fundamental interests." Thus, "it is important to shape circumstances before crises emerge, and to meet threats before they become dire."[5] Signatories to these principles and other PNAC supporters dominated the Bush administration's foreign policy team, including Paul Wolfowitz, Richard Perle, Donald Rumsfeld, Dick Cheney, Elliott Abrams, Lewis Libby, and John R. Bolton.[6]

The core themes of the DPG draft and related themes were developed in great detail in PNAC's report, "Rebuilding America's Defenses" (RAD).[7] Published a year before the terrorist attacks of 9/11, RAD was a sweeping blueprint for U.S. global domination through the unilateral use of military power. In "broad terms, we saw the project as building upon the defense strategy outlined by the Cheney Defense Department," the authors of RAD wrote. "The Defense Policy Guidance (DPG) drafted in the early months of 1992 provided *a blueprint for maintaining preeminence*, precluding the rise of a great power rival, and shaping the international security order in line with American principles and interests." The "basic tenets of the DPG, in our judgment, remain sound."

The Soviet Union no longer existed, and no nation or group of nations was capable of restraining U.S. power. "The Cold War world was a bipolar world; the 21st century is—for the moment, at least—decidedly unipolar, with America as the world's 'sole superpower,'" RAD stated. "At no time in history has the international security order been as conducive to American interests and ideals. The challenge for the coming century is to preserve and enhance this 'American peace.'" A fundamental premise of RAD was "that U.S. military capabilities should be sufficient to support *an American grand strategy committed to building upon this unprecedented opportunity.*" Although at "present the United States faced no global rival," RAD warned that "even a global *Pax Americana* will not preserve itself," and that "unless the United States maintains sufficient military strength, this opportunity will be lost." "*America's grand strategy,*" RAD argued, "should aim to preserve and extend this advantageous position as far into the future as possible."

The grand strategy sought to capitalize on and make permanent the strategic advantages afforded by present military supremacy. "America should seek to preserve and extend its position of global leadership by maintaining the preeminence of U.S. military forces," RAD said. "Preserving the desirable strategic situation in which the United States now finds itself *requires a globally preeminent military capability both today and in the future.*" It needed "a military that is strong and ready to meet both present and future challenges; a foreign policy that boldly and purposefully promotes American principles abroad; and national leadership that accepts the United States' global responsibilities." Significant increases in military spending were required, RAD argued. Thus the United States would have the capabilities to "fight and decisively win multiple, simultaneous major theater wars"; "perform the 'constabulary' duties associated with shaping the security environment in critical regions"; "maintain nuclear strategic superiority"; "develop and deploy global missile defenses . . . to provide a secure basis for U.S. power projection around the world"; and "insure the long-term superiority of U.S. conventional forces."

"Fulfilling these requirements is essential if America is to retain its militarily dominant status for the coming decades," RAD declared. Not fulfilling them could mean "the loss of a global security order that is uniquely friendly to American principles and prosperity." Without dramatic increases in U.S. military spending, aggressive deployment of U.S. forces abroad, and accelerated development of new weapons systems, including the militarization of space, it would be impossible "to maintain the United States as the *'arsenal of democracy'* for the 21st century."

RAD also made the case for preventive war or so-called preemption, the idea that the United States had the right to attack others whenever they threatened U.S. interests or might threaten them in the future. It "is important to shape circumstances before crises emerge, and to meet threats before they become dire," it said. "Today . . . security can only be acquired at the 'retail' level by deterring or, when needed, by compelling regional foes to act in ways that protect American interests and principles." As former Vice President Al Gore explained:

> What they meant by preemption was not the inherent right of any nation to act preemptively against an imminent threat to its national security, but rather an exotic new approach that asserted a unique and unilateral U.S. right to ignore international law wherever it wished to do so and take military action against any nation, even in circumstances where there was no imminent threat. All that is required, in the view of Bush's team, is the mere assertion of a possible, future threat—and the assertion need be made by only one person, the President.[8]

RAD shifted U.S. strategic doctrine away from containment and deterrence to offensive war. It criticized prior "Pentagon war-games" for having "given little or no consideration to the force requirements necessary not only to defeat an attack [from North Korea and Iraq] but to remove these regimes from power." Elsewhere it declared that "American armed forces will remain the core of efforts to deter, defeat, or *remove from power* regional aggressors."

The authors of RAD were convinced that military supremacy would allow the United States to expand and secure its interests and to defeat any and all adversaries. They were aware, however, that there were other countries or groups that sought ways to impede the U.S. grand strategy. This interference, of course, was unacceptable to the writers of RAD, who treated it as a sign of hostility that justified preventive war. As Michael Mann observed, "The most fundamental criteria of a rogue state are that the US does not like it, and that it is not too powerful."[9] Without quite saying it, RAD implied that nations seeking weapons of mass destruction were doing so *defensively and rationally*. They were not driven by offensive designs or irrational motives to kill Americans but were rather responding to, and seeking to thwart, U.S. imperial policies. RAD warned that "widespread technological and weapons proliferation are creating a dynamic that may *threaten America's ability to exercise its dominant military power*," and that "adversaries like Iran, Iraq, and North Korea are rushing to develop ballistic missiles and nuclear weapons as *a deterrent to American intervention*."

"These are not offensive weapons," Michael Mann wrote. "Anyone who fired off their warheads against the US would invite total obliteration, so they cannot possibly threaten the US." The reason nuclear weapons were proliferating in the global South, Mann explained, is because "they produce a big deterrence pay-off at relatively low cost. Above all, they seem to protect a state against American imperialism. The US will think twice about attacking a country with established nuclear weapons, they reason."[10]

Yet U.S. leaders were aware of a similar dynamic of reciprocity that linked increased terrorism to U.S. belligerence. When U.S. leaders openly state their intention to dominate the world, establish and flaunt overwhelming military superiority, aggressively use military power to crush resistance, and pursue interests unilaterally while opposing international law, standards, and norms—then they can rightly anticipate more terrorism. In 1998, Presidential Decision Directive 62 stated: "America's unrivaled military superiority means that potential enemies (whether nations or terrorist groups) that choose to attack us will be more likely to resort to terror instead of conventional military assault."[11] In a 1997 report the Defense Science Board had reached a similar conclusion: "Historical data show a strong correlation between U.S. involvement in international situations and an increase in terrorist attacks against the United States. In addition, the military asymmetry that denies nation states the ability to engage in overt attacks against the United States drives the use of transnational actors."[12] In other words, U.S. military power dominates traditional arenas that once were marked by military competition so as to leave adversaries few options other than to engage the United States in asymmetrical conflicts involving nontraditional forms of power, including terrorism.

Unilateralism with a Purpose

The logic behind the war with Iraq and many of the unilateral actions described in the previous chapter become clearer in light of the grand strategy advocated in RAD. For example, the desire to have a free hand and increased capabilities to militarily intervene throughout the world and to militarize and control the Middle East are recurring themes. RAD declared that the "presence of American forces in critical regions around the world is the visible expression of America's status as a superpower." As a superpower with global reach, the United States would need to carry out numerous "constabulary missions" around the world that might not be accepted or legitimized by the international community. The term "constabulary missions" is a euphemism for global sheriff duties; but in the case of the United States, these duties are self-appointed and not designated by the authority of others. RAD observed that these "constabulary missions are far more complex and likely to generate violence than traditional 'peacekeeping' missions." Such missions demand "American political leadership rather than that of the United Nations," which RAD claimed was ineffective. "Nor can the United States assume a UN-like stance of neutrality; the preponderance of American power is so great and its global interests so wide that it cannot pretend to be indifferent to the political outcome" in the Persian Gulf and elsewhere.

RAD stated that the "trend is for a larger U.S. security perimeter, bringing with it new kinds of missions." This meant more "constabulary missions" in strategically important areas. In "the Persian Gulf region," RAD acknowledged, "the presence of American soldiers . . . has become a semi-permanent fact of life." "Indeed, the United States has for decades sought to play a more permanent role in Gulf regional security. While the unresolved conflict with Iraq *provides the immediate justification*," RAD explained, "the need for a substantial American force presence in the Gulf transcends the issue of the regime of Saddam Hussein."

A major objective of the United States during the first Gulf War (1991) was to establish a permanent military ground presence in the region, including in Saudi Arabia. The U.S. success in doing so motivated Osama bin Laden to orchestrate terrorist attacks targeting the United States. RAD, written a year before 9/11, reported a "geometric increase in the presence of U.S. armed forces" in the "Persian Gulf and surrounding region" since the end of the Cold War. The "presence of American ground forces and land-based air forces in the region mark a notable shift from the 1980s, when naval forces carried the overwhelming burden of U.S. military presence in the region." According to RAD, the United States retained "what amounts to a near-permanent land force in Kuwait." Although "Saudi domestic sensibilities demand that the forces based in the Kingdom nominally remain rotational forces, it has become apparent that this is now a semi-permanent mission."

The presence of U.S. forces and semipermanent bases created problems for governments in the region because it fueled popular resentments. RAD said, for example, that the "Air Force presence in the Gulf region is a vital one for U.S. military strategy, and the United States should consider it a *de facto* permanent presence, even as it seeks ways to lessen Saudi, Kuwaiti and regional concerns about the U.S. presence." Despite popular resentment, RAD recommended that "*a permanent unit [of the U.S. Army] be based in the Persian Gulf Region.*" No one who read "Rebuilding America's Defenses" would be surprised that within weeks of the U.S. invasion of Iraq, the United States began constructing four new military bases there.

Another dominant theme in RAD that sheds light on unilateralist policies discussed previously is the determination to militarize and control space. RAD acknowledged that "American land power remains the essential link in the chain that translates U.S. military supremacy into American geopolitical preeminence." It also recognized that "the increasing sophistication of American air power" allows it to "attack any target on earth with great accuracy and virtual impunity," Nevertheless, RAD placed great emphasis on U.S. domination of space. Militarization of space was central to the grand strategy of achieving global domination because it was the key to establishing and maintaining *permanent* military supremacy.

RAD stated that "maintaining control of space will inevitably require *the application of force both in space and from space,* including but not limited to antimissile defenses and defensive systems capable of protecting U.S. and allied satellites; space control cannot be sustained in any other fashion, with conventional land, sea, or air force, or by electronic warfare." It said that "space dominance may become so essential to the preservation of American military preeminence that it may require a separate service." According to the authors of RAD:

> In short, the unequivocal supremacy in space enjoyed by the United States today will be increasingly at risk. As Colin Gray and John Sheldon have written, "Space control is not an avoidable issue. It is not an optional extra." For U.S. armed forces to continue to assert military preeminence, control of space—defined by Space Command as "the ability to assure access to space, freedom of operations within the space medium, and an ability to deny others the use of space"—must be an essential element of our military strategy. If

America cannot maintain that control, its ability to conduct global military operations will be severely complicated, far more costly, and potentially fatally compromised.

Dominating space was the lynchpin of its grand strategy of global domination through military supremacy. RAD identified two vital components for dominating space: positioning weapons in space and deployment of an antiballistic missile system. RAD declared that "effective ballistic missile defense will be the central element in the exercise of American power and the projection of U.S. military forces abroad. Without it," RAD warned, "weak states operating small arsenals of crude ballistic missiles, armed with basic nuclear warheads or other weapons of mass destruction, will be . . . in a strong position to deter the United States from using conventional force. . . . America's ability to project power will be deeply compromised." "The failure to build missile defenses" would "compromise the exercise of American power abroad," which would "ensure that the current *Pax Americana* comes to an early end."

Formalization

"America's grand strategy" for global domination laid out in RAD was blatantly imperial and politically unrealistic. The authors of RAD indicated that "the process of transformation, even if it brings revolutionary change, is likely to be a long one, absent some catastrophic and catalyzing event—like a new Pearl Harbor." The terrorist attacks of 9/11 fit the bill perfectly, allowing them to implement predetermined policies amid the politics of fear they cultivated. Under the fearful shadow of 9/11 the Bush administration enshrined "America's grand strategy" as formal policy in "The National Security Strategy of the United States of America" (NSS) issued by President Bush in September 2002.

Today the United States enjoys a position of unparalleled military strength and great economic and political influence. In keeping with our heritage and principles, we do not use our strength to press for unilateral advantage. We seek instead to create a balance of power that favors human freedom: conditions in which all nations and all societies can choose for themselves the rewards and challenges of political and economic liberty. In a world that is safe, people will be able to make their own lives better. We will defend the peace by

fighting terrorists and tyrants. We will preserve the peace by building good relations among the great powers. We will extend the peace
by encouraging free and open societies on every continent.[13]

This high-sounding rhetoric collapsed within the text itself. The NSS,
like the DPG and RAD predecessor documents to which it was indebted,
revealed a dangerous, arrogant will to power. "It is time to reaffirm the
essential role of American military strength," the NSS stated. "We must
build and maintain our defenses beyond challenge." The U.S. must seek to
"dissuade future military competition." "The unparalleled strength of the
United States forces, and their forward deployment" demonstrated
"resolve to maintain a balance of power that favors freedom." The NSS
offered this limited but revealing definition of freedom: "If you can make
something that others value, you should be able to sell it to them. If others
make something that you value, you should be able to buy it. This is real
freedom, the freedom for a person—or a nation—to make a living." "The
United States," therefore, was committed to bringing "free markets, and
free trade to every corner of the world."

The NSS, like RAD, sought dramatic increases in military spending and
expansion of U.S. bases worldwide in order to increase interventionist
capabilities. In order "to meet the many security challenges we face, the
United States will require bases and stations within and beyond Western
Europe and Northeast Asia, as well as temporary access arrangements for
the long-distance deployment of U.S. forces." "Our forces will be strong
enough to dissuade potential adversaries from pursuing a military build-
up in hopes of surpassing, or equaling, the power of the United States."

The NSS also formalized RAD's views on preventive war, militarization
of space, and U.S. unilateralism. The United States was "prepared to act
apart when our interests and unique responsibilities require." It would pursue its interests through "coalitions of the willing." "We will build defenses
against ballistic missiles and other means of delivery. . . . And, as a matter of
common sense and self-defense, America will act against such emerging
threats before they are fully formed. We cannot defend America and our
friends," the NSS stated, "by hoping for the best." "While the United States
will constantly strive to enlist the support of the international community,
we will not hesitate to act alone, if necessary, to exercise our right of self-
defense by acting preemptively." We will take "anticipatory action to defend
ourselves. . . . To forestall or prevent . . . hostile acts by our adversaries, the
United States will, if necessary, act preemptively."

The NSS elevated the idea of preventive war to the level of official foreign policy doctrine, although the Bush administration referred to it as "preemptive" war.[14] The U.S Department of Defense *Quadrennial Defense Review Report* (QDR) released on September 30, 2001, foreshadowed a "preemptive" war with Iraq. It called for military capabilities sufficient to "swiftly defeat aggression in overlapping major conflicts while preserving for the President the option to call for a decisive victory in one of these conflicts—including the possibility of regime change or occupation."[15] Arthur Schlesinger, historian and former adviser to the Kennedy administration, wrote at the time of the U.S. invasion of Iraq: "The president has adopted a policy of 'anticipatory self-defense' that is alarmingly similar to the policy that imperial Japan employed at Pearl Harbor, . . . [and] today it is we Americans who live in infamy."[16]

The unilateralism advocated in the DPG draft and RAD and formalized in the NSS and QDR was born of necessity. Neither allies nor adversaries lent credence or international legitimacy to a U.S. grand strategy aimed at establishment of a permanent global empire. The United States was determined to invade Iraq, establish a compliant government, and take control of Iraqi oil. It was also eager to establish permanent military bases in Iraq in order to control Middle Eastern oil as part of a broader effort to control global energy supplies and their suppliers.

The report of the National Energy Policy Development Group released in May 2001—known as the Cheney report, after its principal author—developed a blueprint for satisfying U.S. energy needs over the next several decades. The United States, according to the report, would become increasingly dependent on imports of petroleum from foreign suppliers. It would need to import 60 percent more petroleum in 2020 than it did in 2001. Over that same period the percentage of petroleum coming from imports was expected to increase from 52 percent to 66 percent. The Cheney report advocated that the White House make securing access to foreign imports "a priority of our trade and foreign policy." This had implications for U.S. policies in oil-producing regions and countries worldwide, including especially the Middle East, the Caspian Sea basin (strategically located near Afghanistan), Angola, Nigeria, Colombia, Venezuela, and Mexico. As Michael Klare observed:

> Virtually all of the areas identified as potential sources of increased oil supplies are chronically unstable, harbor anti-American sentiments, or both. . . . U.S. efforts to obtain more petroleum from these

countries are almost certain to provoke resistance. . . . There is, then, an unacknowledged *security* dimension to the Cheney plan, with considerable significance for U.S. military policy. An energy policy favoring increased U.S. access to oil reserves in chronically unstable areas such as the Persian Gulf, the Caspian Sea basin, Latin America, and sub-Saharan Africa will prove far more tenable if accompanied by a military strategy favoring a significant enhancement in America's capacity to project military power into these areas.[17]

The invasion of Iraq was the most visible symbol of the convergence between the "grand strategy," oil politics, and determined militarization. It required lies, inflated fears, and unilateral action. The United States tried to cajole but eventually was forced to ignore the United Nations and build a rather pathetic "coalition of the willing" in pursuit of its goal of permanent empire. Michael Ignatieff has written that the concentration of oil in the Gulf "makes it what a military strategist would call the empire's center of gravity."[18] "Iraq is the ONLY country in the world with sufficient reserves to balance Saudi Arabia," Michael Klare wrote. "By occupying Iraq and controlling its government, the United States will solve its long-term oil-dependency dilemma for a decade or more. And this, I believe," Klare said, "is a major consideration in the administration's decision making about Iraq."[19]

Klare pointed out that "maintenance of a stranglehold over Persian Gulf oil is also consistent with the administration's declared goal of attaining permanent military superiority over all other nations." He wrote:

If you read administration statements on U.S. national security policy, you will find that one theme stands out above all others: the United States must prevent any potential rival from ever reaching the point where it could compete with the United States on something resembling equal standing. . . . One way to accomplish this . . . is to pursue advances in technology that allow the United States to remain ahead of all potential rivals in military systems. . . . Another way to do this is maintain a stranglehold on the economy of potential rivals, so that they will refrain from challenging us out of fear of being choked to death through the denial of vital energy supplies. . . . As I see it, then, the removal of Saddam Hussein and his replacement with someone beholden to the United States is a key part of a broader U.S. strategy aimed at assuring permanent American global dominance.[20]

Unilateralism with a purpose is also evident in U.S. actions precipitated by its commitment to militarize space as part of its grand strategy. The United States is a signatory and was the principal author of the Outer Space Treaty of 1967. That treaty recognized "the common interest of all mankind in the progress of the exploration and use of outer space for peaceful purposes."[21] Nearly every nation in the world is on record as opposing the militarization of space. Unilateral action was needed to overcome these "obstacles" to the grand strategy.

RAD admitted that "a space-based system would violate the ABM Treaty," and that "the Clinton Administration's adherence to the 1972 ABM Treaty has frustrated development of useful ballistic missile defenses." The solution adopted by the Bush administration was to withdraw from the Treaty. The "Report of the Commission to Assess United States National Security, Space Management, and Organization" (known as the Rumsfeld Commission) also tried to circumvent existing agreements. It claimed that the United States had to redefine "peaceful" and reshape "the legal and regulatory environment" concerning weapons in space. It said:

The U.S. and most other nations interpret "peaceful" to mean "non-aggressive"; this comports with customary international law allowing the routine military activities in outer space. . . . There is no blanket prohibition in international law on placing weapons in space, applying force from space to earth or conducting military operations in and through space. The U.S. must be cautious of agreements intended for one purpose that, when added to a larger web of treaties and regulations, may have unintended consequences of restricting future activities in space.[22]

According to the Rumsfeld Commission, "Reality indicates that space" will become a realm of conflict. "Given this virtual certainty, the U.S. must develop the means both to deter and to defend against hostile acts in and from space. This," the report stated, "will require superior space capabilities." "Space-related capabilities help national leaders to implement American foreign policy and, when necessary, to use military power in ways never before possible." "In the coming period," the report stated, "the

U.S. will conduct operations to, from, in and through space in support of national interests both on earth and in space."[23]

The "Air Force Space Command's Strategic Master Plan FY04 and Beyond" declared similarly that the "Air Force Space Command has the vision and the people to ensure [that] the United States achieves Space Superiority today and in the future." "We are developing capabilities to control space and maintain our Space Superiority." The Space Command was developing "space power options to discourage . . . any form of coercion against the United States." "Our strategy is to maintain and increase the advantages of our force-enabling capabilities while expanding our role as a full-spectrum force provider with new capabilities to deny the advantages of space to our adversaries," the Master Plan said. "Our strategy will enable us to transform space power to provide our Nation with diverse options to globally apply force in, from, and through space with modern ICBMs, offensive counterspace, and new conventional prompt global strike capabilities."[24]

The objectives to be pursued through the militarization and control of space were stated clearly in the United States Space Command report "Vision 2020." The cover of "Vision 2020" featured a laser shot from space destroying a target on earth overlaid with the caption: "US Space Command—dominating the space dimensions of US military operations to protect US interests and investments. Integrating Space Forces into warfighting capabilities across the full spectrum of conflict." "Vision 2020" described domination of space as vital to U.S. intervention capabilities in a world that was fracturing due to inequalities resulting from globalization. "Although unlikely to be challenged by a global peer competitor, the United States will continue to be challenged regionally. The globalization of the world economy will also continue, with a widening between the 'haves' and 'have-nots.'"[25] Ironically, through the lens of "Vision 2020" we are able to clearly see U.S. imperial ambitions.

Much of what I have written concerning links between unilateralism and the U.S. desire to militarize space also applies to U.S. nuclear ambitions. The United States had to go it alone and violate existing agreements in order to move forward on a new strategic nuclear agenda. The Nuclear Posture Review submitted to Congress on December 31, 2001, targeted a broad range of potential adversaries for nuclear attack, including China, Iran, Iraq, Russia, Syria, North Korea, and Libya. It called for development of "nuclear offensive forces" as part of a "capabilities approach" to nuclear weapons and raised the possibility of development of a new generation of lower-yield systems. It also raised the specter of nuclear weapons deployed in space as part of a multi-tiered missile defense system.[26]

Double standards proliferate. The United States selectively threatens war against nations who pursue or threaten to pursue development of nuclear, biological, or chemical weapons systems. Yet it modernizes its own systems and refuses to open its own production facilities to international inspection. It sabotages the Chemical Weapons Convention and refuses to ratify the protocol to strengthen the Biological Weapons Convention. It undermines the Biological and Toxins Weapons Convention (BWC) by resisting a legally binding enforcement mechanism. It refuses to ratify the Comprehensive Test Ban Treaty, abrogates the ABM Treaty, and announces early deployment of a national missile defense system (NMD). If NMD becomes effective, U.S. leaders claim it would be a shield from which the United States could project power and carry out *offensive* war with impunity. "The US is the greatest possessor of WMDs, and it is also the greatest proliferator of highly destructive weapons through its massive arms sales abroad," Michael Mann wrote. "The US naturally has no intention of disarming itself," and yet the "US itself constitutes the biggest threat of nuclear proliferation."[27] It is little wonder that the United States is resented by many and understood to be a grave threat to peace.

Impunity with Immunity

"America's grand strategy" for militarized empire also places into context U.S. hostility to the International Criminal Court (ICC). The United States acts with impunity but demands immunity. Seeking global domination through military power, disdaining international law, ignoring the Geneva Conventions, undermining the United Nations, acting alone, opposing protocols proscribing torture, enshrining the dangerous idea of preventive war as official doctrine, and sending U.S. soldiers on "constabulary missions" to control oil and other resources—all these inevitably involve U.S. soldiers and U.S. leaders in serious breaches of international law. By objective standards, as opposed to standards determined under the rubric of exceptionalism, U.S. leaders and U.S. soldiers should be subject to and accountable for crimes against humanity, genocide, or crimes of war as defined by the Nuremberg Principles, the Geneva Conventions, and the 1984 Convention against Torture. The U.S. leaders fear this and therefore have sought to cripple the ICC.

The National Security Strategy of the United States stated: "We will take the actions necessary to ensure that our efforts to meet our global security commitments and protect Americans are not impaired by the potential investigations, inquiry, or prosecution by the International Criminal Court (ICC), whose jurisdiction does not extend to Americans and which we do not accept."[28] It also expressed the U.S. government's determination to "implement fully the American Servicemembers Protection Act, whose provisions are intended to ensure and enhance the protection of U.S. personnel and officials."[29] Human Rights Watch dubbed this the "Hague Invasion Act" and described it this way:

> U.S. President George Bush today [August 3, 2002] signed into law the American Servicemembers Protection Act of 2002, which is intended to intimidate countries that ratify the treaty for the International Criminal Court (ICC). The new law *authorizes the use of military force to liberate any American citizen of a U.S. allied country being held by the court,* which is located in the Hague. . . . In addition, the law provides for the withdrawal of U.S. military assistance from countries ratifying the ICC treaty, and restricts U.S. participation in United Nations peacekeeping unless the United States obtains immunity from prosecution.[30]

Not surprisingly, before turning "sovereignty" over to Iraq in June 2004, the Bush administration took "the unusual step of bestowing on its troops and personnel immunity from prosecution by Iraqi courts for killing Iraqis or destroying local property after the occupation ends." This extended an order that had been in place throughout the occupation of Iraq.[31]

During the Bush administration the United States, according to its own definition, took on the character of a rogue state. Rogue states, according to the NSS, had the following attributes: They "brutalize their own people and squander their national resources for the personal gain of the rulers." They "display no regard for international law, threaten their neighbors, and callously violate international treaties to which they are a party." They "sponsor terrorism around the globe." And they "are determined to acquire weapons of mass destruction, along with other advanced military technology, to be used as threats or offensively to achieve the aggressive designs of these regimes."[32]

The "grand strategy" of the neoconservatives was explicitly imperial. It sought to build a permanent empire by establishing military supremacy and using supremacy as a basis for power projection and control of the world's resources. The empire it inherited and sought to revitalize through its warped vision and destructive policies, however, was an empire already in crisis. The costs of U.S. Empire have been high for many decades. The imperial fantasies and policies of the Bush administration weakened the empire further while dramatically escalating the negative costs borne by citizens and noncitizens alike.

Notes

1. The National Security Strategy of the United States of America, The White House, September 2002, 29.

2. Michael Klare, "Resources," in *Power Trip: U.S. Unilateralism and Global Strategy after September 11* (ed. John Feffer; New York: Seven Stories, 2003), 60.

3. "Excerpts from 1992 Draft 'Defense Planning Guidance,'" www.pbs.org/wgbh/pages/frontline/shows/iraq/etc/wolf.html.

4. Quoted in Benjamin R. Barber, *Fear's Empire: War, Terrorism, and Democracy* (New York: W. W. Norton, 2003), 96.

5. Quotes from the Project for the New American Century "Statement of Principles," PNAC, 1150 Seventeenth St. NW, Suite 510, Washington, DC 20036.

6. For a more exhaustive list, see Feffer, *Power Trip*, 205–9.

7. The Project for the New American Century was established in 1997. "From its inception, the Project has been concerned with the decline in the strength of America's defenses, and in the problems this would create for the exercise of American leadership." This and all other quotes in this section are from "Rebuilding America's Defenses: Strategy, Forces and Resources for a New Century," A Report of The Project for the New American Century, September 2000. Italicized phrases indicate emphasis I have added with the exception of their reference to Pax Americana.

8. "Remarks by Al Gore," as prepared, New York University, May 26, 2004, http://www.moveonpac.com/goreremarks052604.html.

9. Michael Mann, *Incoherent Empire* (London: Verso, 2003), 195.

10. Ibid., 30.

11. "Combatting Terrorism: Presidential Decision Directive 62," May 22, 1998, www.nbcindustrygroup.com/0522pres3.htm.

12. Quoted in Chalmers Johnson, *Blowback: The Costs and Consequences of American Empire* (New York: Metropolitan Books, Henry Holt, 2000), 9.

13. The National Security Strategy of the United States of America, The White House, September 2002.

14. "Preemptive war" is understood to reflect a nation's right to engage in war if it knows it is about to be invaded or attacked. For example, if an enemy's planes are in the air on their way to bomb your nation, you have the right to shoot them down before they reach your borders. "Preventive war" is based on the idea that a nation has the right to unilaterally decide to attack others whenever it decides that a group

or nation may now or at some time in the future threaten your interests. The Bush administration used the language of preemption, but its actual policies reflected the idea of preventive war.

15. U.S. Department of Defense, Quadrennial Defense Review Report, 30 September 2001, 2.

16. Quoted in John Ikenberry, "America's Imperial Ambition," *Foreign Affairs,* September–October, 2002.

17. Michael Klare, "Resources," 53–54 (emphasis in original).

18. Michael Ignatieff, "The Burden," *New York Times Magazine,* January 5, 2003.

19. Michael T. Klare, "The Coming War with Iraq: Deciphering the Bush Administration's Motives," *Foreign Policy in Focus,* January 16, 2003. http://www.fpif.org/pdf/gac/0301warreasons.pdf.

20. Ibid.

21. "Treaty on Principles Governing the Activities of States in the Exploration and Use of Outer Space, Including the Moon and Other Celestial Bodies," signed at Washington, London, Moscow, January 27, 1967, and entered into force October 10, 1967.

22. "Report of the Commission to Assess United States National Security, Space Management, and Organization," January 11, 2001.

23. Ibid.

24. "Air Force Space Command's Strategic Master Plan FY04 and Beyond," October 28, 2002.

25. "The United States Space Command Vision 2020," http://www.fas.org/spp/military/docops/usspac/visbook.pdf.

26. See "Nuclear Posture Review," excerpts, www.globalsecurity.org/wmd/library/policy/dod/npr.htm. Also see William Hartung, "Military," in *Power Trip* (ed. Feffer), 67–70.

27. Mann, *Incoherent Empire,* 30, 37.

28. The National Security Strategy of the United States of America, The White House, September 2002, 31.

29. Ibid.

30. "U.S.: 'Hague Invasion Act' Becomes Law," *Human Rights News,* August 3, 2002 (emphasis added).

31. Robin Wright, "U.S. Troops in Iraq Granted Immunity," *Minneapolis Star Tribune,* June 24, 2004.

32. The National Security Strategy of the United States of America, 14.

4

EMPIRE WITHOUT EXCEPTION

We have only just begun our confrontation with our imperial history, our imperial ethic, and our imperial psychology.

—William Appleman Williams[1]

The imperial project of the so-called neoconservatives is not conservatism at all but radicalism, egotism, and adventurism articulated in the stirring rhetoric of traditional patriotism.

—Clyde Prestowitz[2]

Our only chance is to talk straight to ourselves and not flinch.

—William Appleman Williams[3]

Rhetoric

"America's grand strategy" was dressed in grandiose rhetoric, and its will to power was presented as benevolent service to the world through enlightened militarism. Benevolence reflected our exceptional character, which justified our military power. Extraordinary evil required as much power as we could muster, which warranted permanent military supremacy and unilateral activism. This kindly veneer covered imperial ambitions. It comforted many citizens and held them captive even as their communities were drained of resources and mobilized for permanent war. The class dimensions of empire went unnoticed: it was "our" benevolence, "our" exceptional character, "our" mission, "our" soldiers, "our" nation, "our" war," "our" divine call. The grand strategy, however, stood naked before much of the world and a growing number of U.S. citizens. Stripped of its veneer of decency, its vision was blatantly arrogant, its objectives transparently imperial, and its consequences horribly destructive. "Because the ideology of virtuous empire envisions not only American world dominance but the remaking of the world in its image, it is a recipe for conflict and perpetual war," Claes G. Ryn wrote. "The moralistic aggressiveness it inspires is certain to inflame international relations. It is certain to provoke opposition and hostility."[4]

The grand strategy's explicit commitment to establish and utilize military supremacy as the basis for permanent empire *was unusual in its bold honesty if not its ambition.* The carnage it left and leaves in its wake presents citizens with an opportunity and a danger. We have the opportunity to reject empire and build a republic responsible to its own citizens and to the community of nations, of which it is a part. This requires historical honesty. We must be willing to "talk straight to ourselves and not flinch" about how our imperial present fits with our imperial past.

Exception Clauses at Work: Abu Ghraib

Graphic photos showing U.S. soldiers torturing Iraqi prisoners at the Abu Ghraib prison were published in the spring of 2004. Although outrage was widespread, many U.S. leaders, pundits, and citizens minimized their significance in multiple ways by involving a variety of exception clauses. We were told that deplorable "abuses" at Abu Ghraib were not widespread, that they were the result of actions taken by a few "bad apples," that they were confined to a small unit in the Abu Ghraib prison, that they did not reflect prison conditions elsewhere, that they weren't quite bad enough to be considered real torture, and that they may have been justified given the nature of the enemy. The *New York Times,* itself reluctant to call torture by its real name, reported: "Defenders of the operation said the methods stopped short of torture, did not violate American anti-torture statutes, and were necessary to fight a war against a nebulous enemy whose strength and intentions could only be gleaned by extracting information from often uncooperative detainees."[5]

We were also told that President Bush and other administration officials had learned about the prison conditions at Abu Ghraib along with the rest of us when the photos were first published. Although they seemed most upset by the invention of the camera, they also expressed surprise and outrage because the "abuses" were said to be *shockingly out of character with traditional American values and policies.* Once informed, we were told, they acted swiftly to correct the abuses and to hold responsible parties accountable.

Each of these exception clauses functioned as damage control and each was false, including the reluctance to call torture by its real name. The 1984 Convention against Torture, signed by the United States, states:

> For the purposes of this Convention, the term "torture" means any act by which severe pain or suffering, whether physical or mental, is intentionally inflicted on a person for such purposes as obtaining from him or a third person information or a confession, punishing him for an act he or a third person has committed or is suspected of having committed, or intimidating or coercing him or a third person, or for any reason based on discrimination of any kind, when such pain or suffering is inflicted by or at the instigation of or with the consent or acquiescence of a public official or other person acting in an official capacity.[6]

The convention also said: "*No exceptional circumstances whatsoever, whether a state of war or a threat of war, internal political instability or any other public emergency, may be invoked as a justification of torture.*"[7] Also, according to U.S. law (the War Crimes Act), "Whoever, inside or outside the United States, commits a war crime," "defined as a grave breach in any of the international conventions signed at Geneva 12 August 1949, or any protocol to such convention to which the United States is a party," is subject to federal prosecution. If found guilty, such a person "shall be fined under this title or imprisoned for life or any term of years, or both, and if death results to the victim, shall also be subject to the penalty of death."[8]

It is clear that both international and national law posed serious potential legal problems for the Bush administration after it approved interrogation techniques involving torture. Scott Horton, a New York attorney and human rights advocate, wrote in a June 2004 article that there had been a "shocking number of deaths in detention." Cases dated back more than sixteen months, and yet "no investigation has been closed, no one has been punished, and evidence of cover-ups abounds." "Clearly," he wrote, "the problem lies far up the chain of command." The administration had scuttled "restrictions on interrogation practices, apparently including the law's prohibitions on torture and cruel, inhuman and degrading treatment." "All this occurred secretly," he said, "deep inside the administration, while the president proclaimed noble goals driving the war in Iraq."[9] As Human Rights Watch reported, "The horrors of Abu Ghraib were not simply the acts of individual soldiers. Abu Ghraib resulted from decisions made by the Bush administration to cast the rules aside."[10]

In light of their conduct and the policies they approved, U.S. officials should be candidates for prosecution before the International Criminal Court. The Bush administration covered this base by refusing to sign onto the ICC. As cited above, however, the War Crimes Act left them vulnerable to prosecution for crimes against humanity in U.S. federal courts, and they knew it. In a memo Alberto Gonzales, White House counsel to President Bush, urged the president to declare that the Geneva Convention did not apply to the conflict with al-Qaida and the Taliban. This, Gonzales argued, would "substantially reduce the threat of domestic criminal prosecution under the War Crimes Act."[11] Rosa Ehrenreich, a former senior adviser to the State Department's Bureau of Human Rights, Democracy, and Labor, summarized the implications of the memo:

> If we reduce the legal arguments in the Gonzales memo to their essential core, we have the president's own lawyer acknowledging that future federal prosecutors might take the view that the actions the administration planned to authorize are war crimes under U.S. law. We then have Gonzales urging the president to help U.S. officials evade future criminal charges by asserting that the Geneva Conventions don't bind the United States.[12]

Exception clauses have far-reaching consequences. In the case of Abu Ghraib, they soft-pedaled torture and blinded us to the policies and policy makers behind the torture and other human-rights violations. More generally, however, exception clauses prevent any meaningful challenge to foundational myths of benevolence and to the real nature of the empire those myths serve. The exception clause saying that torture at Abu Ghraib is the product of a few bad apples is but one point on an exceptionalist continuum. Positioned at a different point on the same continuum is the claim that such "abuse" is completely out of character with traditional U.S. foreign policy tactics, goals, and values. Neither exception clause survives careful scrutiny as Iraqis, Salvadorans, Chileans, Iranians, Afghans, detainees at Guantanamo Bay, and many others know from wounds in their own flesh.

Without Exception

Let us consider several historical examples from the Philippines and Central America that stretch over a period of nearly a hundred years in which U.S. foreign policy was specifically linked to terror and torture not unlike that connected to the U.S. occupation of Iraq. Claes G. Ryn wrote concerning the Bush administration that "the will to power almost always presents itself as benevolent concern for others," and that the "desire for empire is thus accompanied by a noble-sounding ideology for how to make the world better." If "by sheer coincidence, this benevolence has the effect of increasing the power of the allegedly virtuous reformer,"[13] Ryn could just as easily have been referring to U.S. leaders and the Philippines a century earlier.

President McKinley told a group of ministers visiting the White House how he came to his decision to invade the Philippines. "I went down on my knees and prayed Almighty God for light and guidance," he told them. McKinley realized that "there was nothing left for us to do but to take them all and to educate the Filipinos, and uplift and civilize and Christianize them, and by God's grace do the very best we could by them, as our fellow men for whom Christ also died." In the Senate in 1900, Senator Albert Beveridge similarly described the takeover of the Philippines as a divine mission: "We will not renounce our part in the mission of our race, trustee, under God, of the civilization of the world."

This sounds very much like George W. Bush. Beveridge also sounded notes similar to the architects of the grand strategy when he acknowledged more base motives for military adventurism. He declared that "the times call for candor" and proceeded to claim that the "Pacific is our ocean" and that the "Philippines are ours forever. . . . And just beyond the Philippines are China's illimitable markets. We will not retreat from either." "It has been charged that our conduct of the war has been cruel," Beveridge said. He then reminded his colleagues "that we are not dealing with Americans or Europeans. We are dealing with Orientals."[14]

In 1901, a correspondent for the Philadelphia Ledger reported from Manila just how cruel the war to "civilize," "Christianize," and "uplift" the Filipinos had become:

> The present war is no bloodless, opéra bouffe engagement; our men have been relentless, have killed to exterminate men, women, children, prisoners and captives, active insurgents and suspected people

from lads of ten up, the idea prevailing that the Filipino as such was little better than a dog. . . . Our soldiers have pumped salt water into men to make them talk, and have taken prisoners people who held up their hands and peacefully surrendered, and an hour later, without an atom of evidence to show that they were even *insurrectos,* stood them on a bridge and shot them down one by one, to drop into the water below and float down, as examples to those who found their bullet-loaded corpses.[15]

An American general reported on the situation in southern Luzon:

One-sixth of the natives of Luzon have either been killed or have died of the dengue fever in the last few years. The loss of life by killing alone has been very great, but I think not one man has been slain except where his death has served the legitimate purposes of war. It has been necessary to adopt what in other countries would probably be thought of as harsh measures.[16]

El Salvador provides a second example that further undermines the myth that torture at Abu Ghraib was exceptional and thus dramatically at odds with the values and conduct of U.S. foreign policy elsewhere. This example is closer to me personally because it corresponds to a period (the 1980s) in which I lived and worked in Central America and involves people whom I had met (murdered Jesuit priests). In the 1980s the U.S.-backed governments throughout Latin America routinely persecuted and killed progressive religious workers who embraced liberation theology. Emerging in the midst of and as response to bitter social injustices, liberation theology stressed God's desire and human responsibility to work for justice. It affirmed the dignity of the human person and said the proper measure of political and economic systems was that they foster dignified living. It said that God sided with the oppressed in struggles for justice, and therefore people and institutions of faith should exercise a preferential option for the poor. It understood sin to be rooted in both individual conduct and in the structures of society. It understood the crucifixion of Jesus to be a consequence of his faith, which led Jesus to confront oppressive groups and institutions in first-century Palestine. It affirmed the resurrection as validation of Jesus' life, which Christians were to emulate.[17]

The Reagan administration equated liberation theology with Marxism, and it targeted its practitioners as enemies. As one lay minister told me in

1987, it was "a crime to be a Christian and to demand justice." The Committee of Santa Fe published a report in 1980 that recommended:

> U.S. foreign policy must begin to counter . . . liberation theology as it is utilized in Latin America by the "liberation theology" clergy. . . . Unfortunately, Marxist-Leninist forces have utilized the church as a weapon against private property and productive capitalism by infiltrating the religious community with ideas that are less Christian than communist.[18]

The United States and its Salvadoran allies countered liberation theology with a vengeance. Bracketing a decade of horrific violence were the murders of Archbishop Romero and four U.S. churchwomen in 1980 and the brutal execution of six Jesuit priests in 1989. All were killed by graduates of the same military training school for Latin American soldiers, the U.S. Army School of the Americas (SOA).[19] In 2001 the school's official Web page boasted that although many of its critics "supported Marxism—Liberation Theology—in Latin America" it had been *"defeated with the assistance of the U.S. Army."*[20]

The U.S. drug enforcement agent Celerino Castillo III provided a disturbing account of religious persecution that includes another example of the torture of "prisoners" as official U.S. policy:

> Lt. Col. Alberto Adame, a U.S. military advisor to El Salvador, . . . recommended one of his friends as a firearms instructor. . . . Dr. Hector Antonia Regalado, a San Salvador dentist, was a household name in the country's power corridors. I was shaking hands with "Dr. Death," as he was known in U.S. political circles, the man reputed to be the Salvadoran death squads' most feared interrogator. In El Salvador, he was known simply as "El Doctor." Regalado's prestige among the right wing stemmed from his ability to extract teeth—and information—without anesthesia. I wanted no part of *El Doctor.* I asked Adame if the embassy had approved Regalado as an advisor. He said Col. James Steele, the U.S. Military Group commander in El Salvador, gave Regalado his blessing. The military obviously wanted this man aboard, human rights abuses and all. . . . *El Doctor* harbored a boiling hatred for anything associated with Communism or revolutionaries, and showed particular disdain for the clergy, who sympathized with the peasants.

Castillo described the cynical practices of "Dr. Death," whose superior was SOA graduate and death squad leader Roberto D'Abuisson:

> Regalado painted a vivid picture of the death squads' modus operandi. After watching their intended victims for a few days to learn their movements, a dozen men in two vans would move in for the abduction. They preferred to strike away from the victim's home, bolting through sliding doors on both sides of the van and yanking the person off the street. As the torture began, they wrote down every name their victim cried out. Regalado practiced his impromptu dentistry on the unfortunate captives with a pair of pliers. I could see these doomed, bleeding men, screaming names with faint hope their pain would end if they fed their captors enough future victims. The pain usually ended with a bullet or the edge of a blade. . . . Regalado was convinced the clergy were Communist infiltrators, trained in Cuba to undermine El Salvador. He considered them cowards, hiding behind the cloth as they spread their diseased doctrine to the peasants he loathed. He spoke of personally directing the deaths of several outspoken priests.[21]

The response of the U.S. administration (Bush Senior) to the murder of the Jesuit priests and to human rights atrocities generally is also reminiscent of recent applications of exception clauses. "The Bush Administration has taken the position that the Jesuit murders were a dramatic departure from Salvadoran army policy," the human rights group America's Watch wrote. "In our view, the murders were entirely in keeping with Salvador's ten-year civil war. . . . Those responsible for almost every other instance of egregious abuse against Salvadoran citizens still enjoy absolute immunity."[22] According to an article in the *National Catholic Reporter* (*NCR*), thousands of declassified State Department, Defense Department, and CIA documents showed "that the Reagan White House was fully aware of who ran, funded, and protected the El Salvador death squads in the 1980s, and planned the 1980 death of San Salvador Archbishop Oscar Arnulfo Romero."[23]

The U.S. creation of death squads in Honduras in the 1980s offers an additional challenge to exceptionalist clauses that allow both myths and empire to go unchallenged. A detailed investigation by Gary Cohn and Ginger Thompson of the *Baltimore Sun* confirmed allegations that the United States was intimately connected to death squads and torturers in

Honduras. According to their report, the "CIA was instrumental in training and equipping Battalion 316," a secret army unit that was home to
Honduran death squads:

> The intelligence unit, known as Battalion 316, used shock and suffo-
> cation devices in interrogations. Prisoners often were kept naked
> and, when no longer useful, killed and buried in unmarked graves.
> Newly declassified documents and other sources show that the CIA
> and the U.S. Embassy knew of numerous crimes, including murder
> and torture, yet continued to support Battalion 316 and collaborate
> with its leaders.[24]

At least nineteen of the ranking Honduran officers linked to death
squad Battalion 316 are SOA graduates, including battalion founder General Luis Alonso Discua. José Valle, a former SOA graduate, a member of
Battalion 316 and an admitted torturer, told Father Roy Bourgeois that he
took "a course in intelligence at the School of the Americas." In the course
he saw "a lot of videos which showed the type of interrogation and torture
used in Vietnam. . . . Although many people refuse to accept it," Valle said,
"all this is organized by the U.S. government."[25]

Another troubling feature of this despicable tale is that the U.S. ambassador to Honduras during this period, John Negroponte, was fully aware
of these atrocities, supported them, and tried to cover them up. "Time
and time again during his tour of duty in Honduras from 1981 to 1985,"
the *Baltimore Sun* series reports, "Negroponte was confronted with evidence that a Honduran army intelligence unit, trained by the CIA, was
stalking, kidnapping, torturing and killing suspected subversives."[26] The
article continues:

> Rick Chidester, then a junior political officer in the U.S. Embassy
> in Tegucigalpa, . . . compiled substantial evidence of abuses by
> the Honduran military in 1982, but was ordered to delete most of
> it from the annual human rights report prepared for the State
> Department to deliver to Congress. Those reports consistently
> misled Congress and the public. "There are no political prisoners in
> Honduras," the State Department asserted falsely in its 1983 human
> rights report. The reports to Congress were carefully crafted to
> convey the impression that the Honduran government and mili-
> tary were committed to democratic ideals. It was important not to

confront Congress with evidence that the military was trampling on civil liberties and murdering dissidents. The truth could have triggered congressional action under the Foreign Assistance Act, which generally prohibits military aid to any government that "engages in a consistent pattern of gross violations of internationally recognized human rights."[27]

Allegations that Negroponte suppressed information about human rights atrocities were confirmed in a 1997 CIA Inspector General's report.[28] A source cited in the report explained the deception, saying that reporting corruption, murders, and executions would "reflect negatively on Honduras and not be beneficial in carrying out U.S. policy."[29] It is rather sobering to realize that John Negroponte, arguably an agent of state terror, was appointed United States ambassador to the United Nations just days after the 9/11 terrorist attacks. He led the diplomatic effort for war with Iraq and the so-called war against terrorism and was later appointed U.S. ambassador to Iraq.

Equally sobering is how idealized portraits of despicable leaders distort historical memory and keep dangerous, exceptionalist myths intact. Much of the carnage in Central America just described, including the war against progressive religious workers, was a consequence of U.S. foreign policies during the Reagan administration. The day after the death of the former president, the editorial cartoon in the *Minneapolis Star Tribune* showed a beaming Reagan accompanied by his words: "There can be no greater good than the quest for peace, and no finer purpose than the preservation of freedom."[30] The lead editorial itself called Reagan a "Happy Warrior," whose "sunny disposition and gentle sense of humor seemed to come at the right time in history." Reagan's "unquestioning optimism seemed a tonic to the country's soul." It "was striking to recall how much the man smiled, and what a comforting good humor he brought to his office." "Reagan often said he saw the United States as 'a shining city on a hill.'" He was "unquestioningly an honest promoter of a principled conservatism."[31]

Mythologies die hard. They hurt others and our nation. They feed exceptionalist impulses and satisfy empire. A report in the *National Catholic Reporter* puts Reagan's "sunny disposition" and "principled conservatism" in a different light. Heeding its wisdom could help us reject exception clauses and idealized revisions of history that hold us captive to myths and that prevent us from embracing a much-needed confrontation with destructive empire:

Substantial documentation by human rights organizations and by the United Nations . . . make it clear: U.S. policies and U.S. training of troops from Central America contributed significantly to awful episodes of torture, assassination and other human rights abuses in the region. . . . Truth commissions in Guatemala, El Salvador and elsewhere in Latin America have helped those cultures to come to a certain honest, if not perfect, understanding of the horrors that occurred. We need our own truth commission and full disclosure of the CIA, military and other government agency documents that will shed full light on our role in Central America in recent decades. As much as any of those other countries, we need to take steps to understand our role in their suffering and to seek pardon and reconciliation. We cannot expect accountability from others around the world for acts of violence and terror if we are not willing to scrutinize ourselves.[32]

It is painful to acknowledge that within the history of U.S. foreign policy the torture of prisoners at Abu Ghraib prison was not exceptional. The same is true for the Bush administration's grand strategy. It is a great and grave temptation in the midst of our present imperial crisis to kick our exceptionalist rhetoric into high gear and to see the grand strategy and the destructive foreign policies of the Bush administration as aberrations. By the logic of this deception, our nation *is exceptional* and the Bush administration's commitment to empire was an *exception*. The U.S. Empire did not begin nor will it end with the administration of George W. Bush. "America's grand strategy" for militarized empire was bold, destructive, and controversial, but it is best understood in basic continuity with the past. We can best see *continuity of empire within competing visions of empire* in relation to five stages of U.S. foreign policy visible from the end of World War II to the present.[33]

Notes

1. William Appleman Williams, *Empire as a Way of Life* (New York: Oxford University Press, 1980), xi.

2. Clyde Prestowitz, *Rogue Nation: American Unilateralism and the Failure of Good Intentions* (New York: Basic Books, 2003), 271.

3. Williams, *Empire as a Way of Life*, 14.

4. Claes G. Ryn, *America the Virtuous* (New Brunswick, NJ: Transaction, 2003), 11.

5. "Harsh CIA Methods Cited in Top Qaeda Interrogation," *New York Times,* May 13, 2004.

6. Convention against Torture and Other Cruel, Inhuman or Degrading Treatment or Punishment, G.A. res. 39/46, [annex, 39 U.N. GAOR Supp. (no. 51) at 197, U.N. doc. A/39/51 (1984)], *entered into force* June 26, 1987.

7. Ibid. (emphasis added).

8. Title 18, part 1, chapter 118, sec. 2411—War Crimes, http://www4.law.cornell.edu/uscode/18/2441.html.

9. Scott Horton, "To Honor Troops, Reaffirm the Geneva Conventions," *Minneapolis Star Tribune,* June 6, 2004.

10. "Bush Policies Led to Abuse in Iraq," *Human Rights News,* June 9, 2004, http://www.hrw.org/english/docs/2004/06/09/iraq8785.htm.

11. Quoted in Rose Ehrenreich Brooks, "Congress Must Pursue Possible U.S. Violations," *Minneapolis Star Tribune,* June 6, 2004.

12. Ibid.

13. Ryn, *America the Virtuous,* 4–5.

14. Quoted in Howard Zinn, *A People's History of the United States 1492–Present* (New York: HarperCollins, 1999), 313–14.

15. Ibid., 313.

16. Ibid., 315–16.

17. I wrote about this theology and the U.S. violent response to it in a novel. See Jack Nelson-Pallmeyer, *Harvest of Cain* (Washington, DC: EPICA, 2001).

18. The Committee of Santa Fe, "A New Inter-American Policy for the Eighties," (Washington, DC: Council for Inter-American Security," 1980).

19. I have written two books about the U.S. Army School of the Americas: *School of Assassins: The Case for Closing the School of the Americas and for Fundamentally Changing U.S. Foreign Policy* (Maryknoll, NY: Orbis Books, 1997); and *School of Assassins: Guns, Greed, and Globalization* (Maryknoll, NY: Orbis Books, 2001). For information about the international nonviolent campaign to close the SOA, contact www.soawatch.org.

20. "U.S. Army School of the Americas Frequently Asked Questions," emphasis added.

21. Celerino Castillo III and Dave Harmon, *Powderburns: Cocaine, Contras and the Drug War* (Oakville, ON: Mosaic, 1994), 151–54.

22. America's Watch testimony, January 31, 1990.

23. Arthur Jones, "Haiti, Salvador Links Viewed," *National Catholic Reporter,* November 19, 1993.

24. Gary Cohn and Ginger Thompson, "Unearthed: Fatal Secrets," *Baltimore Sun,* reprint of a series that appeared June 11–18, 1995.

25. *Inside the School of Assassins,* a documentary film produced by Robert Richter, Richter Productions. This hour-long documentary can be ordered from SOA Watch.

26. *Baltimore Sun,* June 11–18, 1995.

27. Ibid.

28. See a commentary by Joseph E. Mulligan "What Did Negroponte Hide and When Did He Hide It?" *Los Angeles Times,* April 19, 2001.

29. Ibid.

30. Steve Sack, *Minneapolis Star Tribune,* June 7, 2004.

31. "Ronald Reagan: Man of Essential Optimism," *Minneapolis Star Tribune,* June 7, 2004.

32. "Discoveries Underline Need for Truth Commission," *National Catholic Reporter,* May 19, 2000.

33. I described four states of U.S. foreign policy in *School of Assassins: Guns, Greed, and Globalization.*

5

CONTINUITY OF EMPIRE

Empire became so intrinsically our American way of life that we rationalized and suppressed the nature of our means in the euphoria of our enjoyment of the ends.

—William Appleman Williams[1]

[Many] aspects of what the American government had done abroad virtually invited retaliatory attacks from nations and peoples who had been victimized. The blowback from the second half of the twentieth century has just begun. In a sense, blowback is simply another way of saying that a nation reaps what it sows. Although individual Americans usually know what they have sown, they rarely have the same knowledge at a national level, since so much of what managers of our empire have done has been kept secret.

—Chalmers Johnson[2]

Stages

Contemporary U.S. Empire can best be understood in relation to five stages in U.S. foreign policy, with stage 1 beginning at the end of World War II and stage 5 encompassing the "grand strategy" of the Bush administration. These stages reveal *shifts in foreign policy strategy and tactics that nonetheless reflect the basic continuity of empire.* By looking at the U.S. Empire in light of foreign policy stages, it is possible to identify how and why the Clinton administration's strategy for empire differed from that of

the Bush administration. It can also help us see that the problem of empire
did not begin with the neoconservatives. Thus, a post-Bush administration
is far more likely to revert to earlier strategies for empire than it is to
undertake the essential task of helping the United States transition from
empire to republic.

Stage 1 (1946–1979)

Post-World War II stage 1 of U.S. foreign policy (roughly 1946–79) was a
period marked by significant U.S. support for repressive militaries and
dictators throughout the so-called Third World. During this period in
Asia alone, U.S.-sponsored dictators included Chiang Kai-shek and his
son Chiang Ching-kuo in Taiwan; Ferdinand Marcos in the Philippines;
Ngo Dinh Diem, Generals Nguyen Khanh, Nguyen Cao Ky, and Nguyen
Van Thieu in Vietnam; General Lon Nol in Cambodia; Marshals Pibul
Songgram, Sarit Thanarat, Praphas Charusathien, and Thanom Kittika-
chorn in Thailand; and General Suharto in Indonesia.[3] More than a dozen
Latin American military dictatorships also ruled with U.S. support during
this period.

The United States relied on Third-World dictators because it was
preoccupied with rebuilding Europe and Japan following World War II
but had significant interests at stake elsewhere. Stable investment climates
were sought and economic interests secured largely through military violence. The chair of Standard Oil warned in 1946 that U.S. private enterprise needed to "strike out and save its position all over the world, or sit by
and witness its own funeral." It had to "assume the responsibility of the
majority stockholder in this corporation known as the world." The goal of
U.S. foreign policy was, he said, to ensure the "safety and stability of our
foreign investments."[4]

That same year the United States opened and began training Latin
American soldiers at the U.S. Army School of the Americas (SOA).
Throughout Latin America the SOA became known as a school of dictators, assassins, and coups. According to Representative Joseph Kennedy's
testimony in 1994 in the *Congressional Record*, it "is a school that has run
more dictators than any other school in the history of the world."[5] A *Los
Angeles Times* editorial urged that the SOA be closed because "it is hard to
think of a coup or human rights outrage that has occurred in [Latin
America] in the past 40 years in which alumni of the School of the Americas were *not* involved."[6]

In 1948 George Keenan clearly articulated the logic and reason why stage 1 of U.S. foreign policy was marked by U.S.-backed dictators and U.S.-supported repressive militaries. Keenan argued that U.S. foreign policy had to be a blunt instrument if the United States was to maintain its privileged position in a world of striking inequalities:

We have about 50 percent of the world's wealth, but only 6.3 percent of its population. . . . In this situation, we cannot fail to be the object of envy and resentment. Our real task in the coming period is to devise a pattern of relationships which will permit us to maintain this position of disparity without positive detriment to our national security. To do so we have to dispense with all sentimentality and day-dreaming; and our attention will have to be concentrated everywhere on our immediate national objectives. We need not deceive ourselves that we can afford today the luxury of altruism and world-benefaction.

Speaking specifically about Asia, but also with relevance for Latin America, Keenan added:

We should cease to talk about vague and . . . unreal objectives such as human rights, the raising of living standards and democratization. The day is not far off when we are going to have to deal in straight power concepts. The less we are hampered by idealistic slogans, the better.[7]

U.S. foreign policy sought to maintain stability while preserving inequalities. It expressed open disdain for development, democracy, and human rights, and therefore not surprisingly relied heavily on repression and violence. Justifying repression became easier as the Cold War heated up. Then, like today, it was standard practice for policy makers to feed noble-sounding, exceptionalist rhetoric to domestic consumers but ignore it in actual practice. The recommendations of a *secret U.S.* government commission report from 1954 must have sounded eerily similar to the Bush administration's internal discussions leading to the decision to "legalize" torture as part of the "war on terror":

It is now clear that we are facing an implacable enemy whose avowed objective is world domination. . . . There are no rules in such a game. Hitherto accepted norms of human conduct do not apply. . . . If the United States is to survive, long-standing American concepts of fair play must be reconsidered. . . . We must learn to subvert, sabotage and destroy our enemies by more clever, sophisticated, more effective methods than those used against us.[8]

Stage 2 (1980–1991)

Stage 2 of U.S. foreign policy (roughly 1980–91) was marked by a *two-track strategy involving military and economic channels of influence.*

Track 1 of stage 2 deepened the repressive violence featured centrally in stage 1. This was evident throughout Central America in the 1980s as the description of religious persecution in El Salvador and death squads in Honduras discussed in chapter 4 made clear. One additional example should be sufficient to illustrate that accelerated repression and violence characterized track 1 of stage 2: U.S. support for the Nicaraguan contras.

A fifty-year U.S.-backed dictatorship was ousted in Nicaragua in 1979 by a revolutionary movement committed to major structural reforms. The United States launched immediately a concerted campaign to destabilize the new government. This campaign included significant training in terrorist tactics for remnants of the former dictator's army, now known as the contras. In 1981 the CIA (U.S. Central Intelligence Agency) director William Casey arranged for Argentina's generals, experienced from a war of terror against their own people in which the United States was also complicit, to train the contras, who set up base camps in Honduras. The U.S. mission in Nicaragua, according to Casey, was to undermine a popular revolution by running the country into the ground. "It takes relatively few people and little support to disrupt the internal peace and economic stability of a small country," he said. Casey knew the U.S.-backed contras might not overthrow the popular Nicaraguan government, but they "will harass the government" and "waste it."[9]

On another occasion Casey told the National Security Council: "We have our orders. I want the economic infrastructure hit, particularly the ports. [If the contras] can't get the job done, we'll use our own people and the Pentagon detachment. We have to get some high-visibility successes."[10] Within months the United States used its own people, known as "Unilaterally Controlled Latino Assets," to blow up an oil pipeline and oil storage tanks. "Although the FDN had nothing whatsoever to do with this operation," former contra leader Edgar Chamorro reported, "We were instructed by the CIA to publicly take responsibility in order to cover the CIA's involvement."[11]

The U.S. Central Intelligence Agency also produced a manual for the contras that encouraged them to assassinate "government officials and sympathizers." The manual, *Psychological Operations in Guerrilla Warfare*, included instructions on "Implicit and Explicit Terror." Terrorizing the populace was important, the manual said, because once the mind of a person "has been reached, the 'political animal' has been defeated, without necessarily receiving bullets. . . . Our target, then, is the minds of the population, all the population: our troops, the enemy troops and the civilian population."[12] "I found many of the tactics advocated in the manual to be offensive," Edgar Chamorro testified to the World Court of Justice. "I complained to the CIA station chief, . . . and no action was ever taken in response to my complaints. In fact," Chamorro continued, "the practices advocated in the manual were employed by the FDN [Fuerza Democrática Nicaragüense, the largest contra group] troops. Many civilians were killed in cold blood. Many others were tortured, mutilated, raped, robbed or otherwise abused."[13]

Chamorro testified that CIA trainers equipped the contras with terrorist training manuals *and* large knives. "A commando knife [was given], and our people, everybody wanted to have a knife like that, to kill people, to cut their throats."[14] His affidavit to the World Court also said:

A major part of my job as communications officer was to work to improve the image of the FDN forces. This was challenging, because it was standard FDN practice to kill prisoners and suspected Sandinista collaborators. In talking with officers in the FDN camps along the Honduran border, I frequently heard offhand remarks like, "Oh, I cut his throat." The CIA did not discourage such tactics. To the contrary, the Agency severely criticized me when I admitted to the press that the FDN had regularly kidnapped and executed agrarian reform workers and civilians. We were told that the only way to defeat the Sandinistas was to . . . kill, kidnap, rob and torture.[15]

Nicaragua took the United States to the World Court in a legal challenge to U.S. aggression. The Court found in favor of Nicaragua and ordered the United States to stop its dirty war and pay Nicaragua billions of dollars in reparations. The United States refused to adhere to the Court's rulings and withdrew from the World Court.

At the same time the United States trained the Nicaraguan contras in terrorist tactics, it also, with the help of the Pakistani Intelligence Agency, recruited and trained radical Islamic fundamentalist extremists and set them to work in Afghanistan. This was "part and parcel of the growth of militarism in the United States," Chalmers Johnson wrote. "The CIA has evolved into the president's private army to be used for secret projects he personally wants carried out (as, for example, in Nicaragua and Afghanistan during the 1980s)."[16] "The Mujahideen received substantial assistance in the form of money, weapons and training from the United States and other foreign powers during the Soviet occupation of Afghanistan," reported Amnesty International USA. "Some of the largest and best-equipped Mujahideen factions that were supported by the United States were made up of Islamist extremists."[17]

The Afghan policy aimed at toppling a pro-Soviet government and draining the Soviet Union of soldiers and money was heralded as a wildly successful strategy. It led to a classic case of blowback, however, as the Islamic extremists morphed into al-Qaida and set their sights on the U.S. Empire for reasons previously discussed.

Track 2 of stage 2 used the International Monetary Fund (IMF) and the World Bank (WB) as instruments of U.S. foreign policy. Structural adjustment programs (SAPs) were imposed on indebted, dependent countries in order to secure U.S. political and economic interests that lie at the heart of U.S. Empire. The standard features of IMF structural adjustment programs included currency devaluations; higher interest rates; strict control of the money supply; cuts in government spending; removal of trade and exchange controls; the use of market forces to set the prices of goods, services, and labor; privatization of public sector enterprises; and export promotion. These measures, according to IMF theory, should result in lower inflation, increased exports, reduced consumption and imports, greater efficiency, international competitiveness, and substantial foreign exchange earnings available for debt servicing. In practice SAPs hurt poor countries in at least seven ways:

- The required emphasis on export production weakened the subsistence sector while strengthening sectors dominated by foreigners.
- When the export requirement was imposed on numerous countries at the same time, it resulted in overproduction and a further deterioration in the terms of trade.

- Higher interest rates mandated by the IMF encouraged speculation, fueled inflation, and aggravated class divisions since credit was limited to the most affluent and powerful economic actors.
- Removal of trade and export controls fostered dependence on foreign inputs, increased the domination of foreign firms over domestic ones, and encouraged capital flight.
- Privatization required by the IMF resulted in greater concentration of wealth and a loss of economic sovereignty.
- Mandated currency devaluations eroded the purchasing power of workers while benefiting foreign corporations operating in export zones.
- Finally, satisfying the IMF and foreign creditors required Third-World governments to drastically reduce government spending with dire consequences for the poor.

According to the United Nations Children's Organization (UNICEF), the world's thirty-seven poorest countries cut health-care budgets by 50 percent and education budgets by 25 percent in the 1980s. UNICEF estimated that more than a million African children died in the 1980s as a result of structural adjustment programs imposed on the poor. In 1988 alone, according to UNICEF, half a million children died in underdeveloped countries as a direct result of SAP-induced austerity measures. "It is essential to strip away the niceties of economic parlance," UNICEF urged, "and say that . . . the developing world's debt, both in the manner in which it was incurred and in the manner in which it is being 'adjusted to' . . . is simply an outrage against a large section of humanity."[18]

Track 2's emphasis on foreign policy through leveraging debt benefited U.S. interests. It ensured a continuous transfer of wealth from poor countries to the United States in the form of interest payments on Third-World debt, and it forced poor countries to integrate their economies into the international system on terms favorable to the United States. Poor majorities suffered greatly, but Third-World elites often benefited from their cooperation with the United States and the international system. "Once a country makes the leap into the system of globalization," Thomas Friedman wrote approvingly, "*its elites begin to internalize this perspective of integration, and always try to locate themselves in a global context.*"[19]

Stage 3 (1992–1997)

Stage 3 of U.S. foreign policy (roughly 1992–97) was a period in which the geopolitical situation allowed economic leverage to largely trump military power. A decade of U.S.-sponsored wars in Central America left Nicaragua destroyed and people throughout the region exhausted and war weary. Structural adjustment programs there and elsewhere had also forced economic changes required by the United States. Most important, the Soviet Union had collapsed, leaving the United States without a military peer and in a position to reshape the world by flexing its economic muscles under the banner of globalization.

During stage 3 of U.S. foreign policy, the Clinton administration sought to build on the "economic successes" of the SAPs imposed throughout the 1980s. The general thrust of stage 3 was to consolidate and exercise influence whenever possible through economic rather than military means. Political and economic benefits from the Third World accrued to the United States throughout stages 1 and 2 as a result of military intervention, repression, supportive dictators, and/or structural adjustment programs. Stage 3 sought to achieve political and economic objectives through legally binding, institutionalized free-trade agreements like the North American Free Trade Agreement (NAFTA) and through international bodies such as the World Trade Organization.

The United States was a lone superpower exercising economic power projection in order to expand its dominance, with globalization rhetoric replacing outdated anti-communism. As Thomas Friedman stated approvingly, in "the globalization system, the United States is now the sole and dominant superpower and all other nations are subordinate to it to one degree or another."[20] U.S. domination of "the globalization system" left most nations, particularly poor ones, with nowhere to turn. Options for all but the most powerful were limited to playing by U.S. rules or not playing at all. A geopolitical climate conducive to economic power projection temporarily lessened the need for military repression. Why send in death squads when you could send in bankers and accomplish similar objectives?

Stage 3 of U.S. foreign policy was marked by accelerated efforts to institutionalize a corporate-led global economic order whose foundations were firmly established through the IMF structural adjustment programs and military repression during earlier stages. A corporate-driven U.S. foreign policy became institutionalized. Power was wielded, less with guns and more through institutions such as the IMF, through trade agreements such as NAFTA and through supracorporate rule-making bodies such as the World Trade Organization (WTO). These became the principal instruments of U.S. foreign policy during stage 3.

Stage 3 foreign policy used global institutions to serve U.S. Empire. The "UN, the World Bank and the IMF," Friedman wrote, "are critical for stabilizing an international system from which America benefits more than any other country."[21] "There are big, important places and there are small unimportant places, and diplomacy is about knowing the difference between the two, and knowing how to mobilize others to act where we cannot or should not go," Friedman wrote. "The very reason we need to support the United Nations and the IMF, the World Bank and the various world development banks is that *they make it possible for the Untied States to advance its interests without putting American lives on the line everywhere, all the time.*"[22] International organizations provided the United States with surrogate troops wearing three-piece suits. Mark Weisbrot writes:

> The IMF is able to tell most governments that if they do not adopt its policies, then they will not get credit from most other sources. This is the most concentrated power in the world, greater in its efficacy than the might of the U.S. military. Very few governments of low- and middle-income countries are strong enough (politically or economically) to stand up to this kind of power. As a result, the United States only rarely needs to use force or the threat of force, because it is able to impose its agenda by means of this cartel.[23]

Thomas Friedman's position with the *New York Times* itself reflected the shift in U.S. foreign policy in stage 3 from military power projection to economic power projection. His new position was created in 1994 to "*cover the intersection between foreign policy and international finance.*"[24] Economic policy planners dominated U.S. foreign policy during the Clinton years. They had an economically driven "grand strategy" that reflected imperial ambitions nearly as grandiose as the Bush administration's military one discussed in the previous chapter. According to Friedman:

> Strategizing has been done by people whom you don't usually associate with grand strategy. Their names are Greenspan [head of the Federal Reserve], Rubin [head of the Treasury Department] and Summers [head of the World Bank]. But don't think just because they did the strategizing, and not the Secretary of State or

the Secretary of Defense, that it does not require a global vision and has not put in place global structures that will fundamentally shape, and hopefully stabilize, relations between states. If that isn't grand strategy, then I don't know what is. If that isn't foreign policy, then I don't know what is.[25]

Stage 4 (1998–2001)

Stage 4 of U.S. foreign policy (roughly 1998 to the advent of the Bush administration in 2001) was also marked by a two-track foreign policy. Shaped during the final years of the Clinton presidency, stage 4 built on and responded to contradictions and limitations encountered in stage 3. It also reflected the resurgent power of the U.S. military-industrial complex.

Track 1 of stage 4 sought to further institutionalize and use economic leverage and economic power as foreign policy engines. It did so through pursuit of additional free trade agreements and through efforts to expand the power and scope of the World Trade Organization.

Thomas Friedman, a strong advocate of a foreign policy grounded in an economically driven "grand strategy," approved of the United States having enormous power because most countries had few realistic choices. They had to accept the dictates of what he called the "Golden Straitjacket" and the "Electronic Herd," by which he meant more or less the conditions set by the IMF and whatever pleased international investors who could move "money around the world with the click of a mouse." The Electronic Herd, Friedman wrote, "gathered in key global financial centers, such as Wall Street, Hong Kong, London and Frankfurt, which I call 'the Supermarkets.' The attitudes and actions of the Electronic Herd and the Supermarkets can have a huge impact on nation-states today, even to the point of triggering the downfall of governments."[26]

In track 2 of stage 4 several factors drove the evident remilitarization of U.S. foreign policy. First, economic leverage was not a suitable means of influence and control in trouble spots such as Colombia or the Persian Gulf. Advocates of an economically driven foreign policy had always understood the importance of military power to U.S. Empire. "Attention, Kmart shoppers," Friedman wrote. "Without America on duty, there will be no America online."[27] They preferred, however, to carry out U.S. foreign policy with economic leverage and believed they could do so effectively in most settings. When they couldn't, and they knew such situations existed, they didn't hesitate to use military muscle. "The struggle for power, the pursuit of material and strategic interests, . . . continue even in a world of microchips, satellite phones, and the Internet," Thomas Friedman wrote. "Globalization does not end geopolitics. Let me repeat that for all the realists who read this book: *Globalization does not end geopolitics.*"[28] The "system of globalization," he declared, depends on "the presence of American power and America's willingness to use that power."

> The hidden hand of the market will never work without a hidden fist. McDonald's cannot flourish without McDonnell Douglas, the designer of the U.S. Air Force F-15. And the hidden fist that keeps the world safe for Silicon Valley's technologies to flourish is called the U.S. Army, Air Force, Navy and Marine Corps. And these fighting forces and institutions are paid for by American taxpayer dollars.[29]

A second factor contributing to the remilitarization of U.S. foreign policy in track 2 of Stage 4 was that corporate-led globalization, the fruit and engine of past economically driven foreign policy "successes," caused and aggravated many serious problems. It increased inequalities and concentrated wealth, accelerated environmental destruction, tore apart cultures, and seriously constricted democracy.[30] SAPs that were imposed on indebted countries during stage 2 of U.S. foreign policy took a brutal toll on the poor. They were institutionalized into a "neoliberal" system, in which globalization was a euphemism for an economic "grand strategy" for empire during stages 3 and 4.

The disastrous consequences of an arrogant "grand strategy" for militarized empire were highly visible during the Bush administration. It is important to see that neoliberalism was imposed on poor nations with similar arrogance and similar consequences. As Michael Mann wrote in *Incoherent Empire*, "To force liberalization on countries before their economies are ready produces disaster." "With the possible exception of Great Britain around 1800," he wrote, "*no modern country has achieved substantial economic development through measures compatible with today's neo-liberalism.*"[31]

Economic power projection was at the heart of U.S. foreign policy during stage 3, and it was featured centrally in track 1 of stage 4. Because its purpose was empire, however, U.S. foreign policy gradually came full circle and increasingly reverted to militarism. Although economic power projection substituted for military intervention for a time, the imperial economic policies it enabled created conditions ripe for social rebellion, which prompted U.S. military responses. "Neo-liberal reforms . . . produce political turmoil and anti-Americanism," Mann wrote. "Not among the rich, who (in the short run) benefit from American policies. But the masses often see them as part of a global economic imperialism in which the rich exploit the masses and the US exploits the rest."[32]

Thomas Friedman acknowledged that the globalization he advocated aggravated inequalities, overwhelmed cultures, and accelerated environmental destruction. He also knew these problems led to uprisings and despair that would need to be countered with military violence in order to defend the dysfunctional system. In "many countries, instead of popular mass opposition to globalization, is wave after wave of crime—people just grabbing what they need." The wars of the future, Friedman wrote would likely be "wars between winners and losers *within* countries."[33]

This dynamic—in which repression gives way to economic leverage only to return to repression as conditions deteriorate—can also be seen in relation to U.S. foreign policy and "democracy." The United States nearly always justifies its intervention with rhetoric about promoting democracy. This rhetoric bears little resemblance to reality, although the issue is sometimes more subtle today than in the past. Recall that for most of stages 1 and 2 the United States and the Third-World governments it supported equated democracy with subversion. As previously explained, U.S. leaders relied on repressive militaries and dictators to seek, establish, or maintain stability. The advent of economic power projection in stages 3 and 4 created possibilities for limited democracy. Elections were in; dictators were out. Civilian governments were in; military governments were out. The parameters for a nation's economy, however, were predetermined and fixed by SAPs, trade rules and agreements, supranational organizations like the WTO, and the profit desires of foreign investors.

Developed and underdeveloped countries, according to Thomas Friedman, had no choice but to accept limited democracy constricted by the market: "On the political front, the Golden Straitjacket narrows the political and economic policy choices of those in power to relatively tight parameters." Put on the Golden Straitjacket, and "your economy grows and your politics shrinks." Its "political choices get reduced to Pepsi or Coke—to slight nuances of taste."[34] The "Electronic Herd gets to vote in all kinds of countries everyday, but those countries don't get to vote on the herd's behavior."[35] As Wharton School globalization expert Stephen J. Kobrin writes, "When the power shifts to these transnational spheres, there are no elections and there is no one to vote for."[36]

Constricted political democracy within limitations determined by the IMF, the "Golden Straitjacket," the "Supermarkets," and the "Electronic Herd" may be a step above Third-World dictatorship, but it is a far cry from authentic democracy. If an economy functions outside the influence of popular politics, then the political arena is reduced to a symbolic, empty shell. It invariably leads to elite sector domination of both politics and the economy. This in turn leads to cynicism about politics.

This process is evident in the United States. where many citizens are disengaged from politics and rarely vote. It is also visible in Latin America, which as Michael Mann observed, "is the most indebted region in the world, and so has experienced the most neo-liberalism." The economic consequences of neoliberalism, which "tends to favor the rich," are predictable. "Structural adjustment programs increase unemployment and widen the gap between rich and poor in poorer countries."[37] The political consequences are also far-reaching. Because Latin American governments are constricted democracies, they are prevented from responding to pressing economic injustices. They make decisions within economic parameters preset by the IMF, trade agreements, and international investors. They cannot stretch the parameters without facing major economic and, if necessary, military reprisals. The result, political paralysis rooted in subservience, breeds disillusionment with democracy itself.

A United Nations study released in April 2004 found that throughout Latin America "democracy does not enjoy good health, fundamentally because it has not provided benefits in terms of reduction of poverty and inequality." According to the head of the United Nations Development Program, "Half of Latin Americans have little faith in democracy due to their frustration." Surveys showed that 56.3 percent of Latin Americans thought economic development was more important than democracy, and 54.7 percent said they would support an authoritarian government if it would resolve their problems.[38]

An economically driven "grand strategy" for empire was nearly as dangerous and costly as its military counterpart discussed in the previous chapter. Contradictions that were rooted in its "successes" eventually required that a military component be upgraded. As Mann explained:

Americans may believe the rhetoric that neo-liberalism works— indeed that free trade and free capital flows are a part of freedom itself. But reality differs. The US aid program is negligible and subordinated to strategic military goals. Neo-liberalism does not bring development to the poorest parts of the world, and it is biased towards the interests of the U.S., the North and the world's wealthy classes. To describe this as benevolent would be self-delusion or hypocrisy. This is not good against evil. On balance it tilts the other way according to most views of morality.[39]

With a few nuances much of what I have written above applies to the situation after the U.S invasion of Iraq. A brutal dictator was supported by the United States during the worst of his abuses, but then alienated his benefactor, lost favor, and was ousted. Many Iraqis, including some who opposed the U.S. invasion, were happy that Saddam Hussein was gone. Unfortunately, however, the objectives of Bush administration officials in Iraq—including establishing permanent military bases, controlling Iraqi oil, and placing other key sectors of Iraq's economy into the hands of their friends and relatives—made real democracy and authentic respect for human rights impossible. Amnesty International's Annual Report of May 2004 surveyed the situation:

> The poor and the marginalized are most commonly denied justice and would benefit most from the fair application of the rule of law and human rights. Yet despite the increasing discourse on the indi-visibility of human rights, in reality economic, social and cultural rights are neglected, reducing human rights to a theoretical con-struct for the vast majority of the world's population. It is no mere coincidence that, in the Iraq war, the protection of oil wells appears to have been given greater priority than the protection of hospitals.[40]

Efforts to directly or indirectly limit and control Iraq's politics and economy in order to service U.S. interests predictably alienated many Iraqis from "democracy" and triggered a backlash that the United States met with even greater repression. Economist Paul Krugman wrote con-cerning what went wrong in Iraq:

> Figures on electricity supply and oil production show a pattern of fitful recovery and frequent reversals; figures on insurgent attacks and civilian casualties show a security situation that got progres-sively worse, not better; public opinion polls show an occupation that squandered the initial goodwill. . . . Let's say the obvious. By making Iraq a playground for right-wing economic theorists, an

employment agency for friends and family, and a source of lucrative contracts for corporate donors, the administration did terrorist recruiters a very big favor.[41]

Remilitarization in Stage 4

Remilitarization in stage 4 of U.S. foreign policy also was driven by a backlash of a different sort: the resurgent power of the U.S. military-industrial-congressional complex that resisted its own downsizing. Within stages 3 and 4, U.S. military spending and policy were largely divorced from any credible threat or vital security need. The collapse of the Soviet Union together with the rise of economic mechanisms for power projection undercut the rationale for high military budgets. The expansion of NATO, accelerated weapons exports, the escalation of the drug war, and money wasted on unworkable missile defense systems—all were disconnected from authentic defense needs. They should be viewed in the context of a desperate search for threats, enemies, and military markets, things on which inflated budgets and wasteful military production depend.

William Hartung, executive director of the World Policy Institute, declared: "The 2000 elections mark an important moment in the transformation of America from a republic in which the military and security forces are subordinated to civilian control, into a garrison state, in which the security of the state and the corporations take precedence over the rights of the individual."[42] This is undoubtedly true. Yet the United States, as Chalmers Johnson has written, long ago moved from having a military responsible for legitimate defense to being a militarized nation. "The nation's armed services come to put their institutional preservation ahead of achieving national security or even a commitment to the integrity of the governmental structure of which they are a part."[43]

The United States was the most militarized country in the history of the world *before* the dramatic military escalation that accompanied the Bush administration's pursuit of a "grand strategy" of global domination through unilateral exercise of military power. Chalmers Johnson wrote that as of "September 2001, the Department of Defense acknowledged [that] at least 725 American military bases existed outside the United States," and there were in fact "many more."[44] "We now station innumerably more uniformed military officers than civilian diplomats, aid workers, or environmental specialists in foreign countries," Johnson reported. This is "a point not lost on the lands to which they are assigned."[45] According to

Amnesty International USA, the United States was training with little accountability "at least 100,000 foreign police and soldiers from more than 150 countries each year." Training took place at "approximately 275 military schools and installations in the United States" as well as on the ground in more than 150 countries.[46] If we factor in the cost of war with Iraq, then U.S. military spending in 2003 and 2004 exceeded that of the rest of the world combined.

Stage 5 (2001–2004)

Stage 5 of U.S. foreign policy began in 2001 with the Bush administration's implementation of the "grand strategy" as discussed previously. Foreign-policy planners in the Clinton and Bush administrations shared two things in common and one important difference. Both sought to strengthen and expand the U.S. Empire, and both believed that the collapse of the Soviet Union removed many of the constraints that once stood in the way of their ambitions. They differed over means. "During the Clinton administration, the United States employed an indirect approach to imposing its will on other nations," Chalmers Johnson wrote. "Clinton camouflaged his policies by carrying them out under the banner of 'globalization.'" "During the 1990s, the rationales of free trade and capitalist economics were used to disguise America's hegemonic power," he stated, "and make it seem benign or, at least, natural and unavoidable. . . . The United States ruled the world," he continued, "but did so in a carefully masked way that produced high degrees of acquiescence among the dominated nations."[47]

The architects and authors of the Bush administration's "grand strategy" considered *the Clinton administration's economically driven strategy for empire* to be wrong-headed and fatally flawed. According to the neoconservatives, overreliance on economic mechanisms and multilateral channels for power projection and empire was ineffectual. President Clinton was squandering a once-in-a-lifetime opportunity for the United States to seize the moment and build a permanent empire rooted in military supremacy. President Bush and the neoconservatives seized the moment to devastating effect, but the means to empire deployed by their predecessors were nearly as destructive as their own.

The five stages of U.S. foreign policy reflect a basic continuity of the U.S. Empire. Grand strategies for empire, whether rooted in economic or military power projection or some combination of both, hurt others worldwide and undermine our republic. An empire based on permanent military supremacy and pursued through unilateral use of military power in service to energy, military, and ideological interests—this is not "our" empire. Similarly, empire pursued through economic power projection that serves the needs of corporate sectors that dominate globalization isn't "our" empire either. As Emmanuel Todd wrote:

> Beyond the shocking images of television "news," it is possible to measure the slowdown of economic growth in the world and the widening of inequalities in both rich and poor countries. These are some of the consequences of economic and financial globalization. They follow logically from the free-market system that makes the working population of every country in the world into global competitors. As a result salaries eventually stop growing or collapse and global demand stagnates.[48]

I prefer living in a republic dotted with windmills than in an empire whose fixation on foreign oil fields dots the global landscape with corpses. I would rather live in a republic where health care is universal and affordable, and where decent wages are received and paid by workers on all sides of borders, than in an empire whose corporations scour the world in search of higher profits based on lowest common denominator wages, destruction of the environment, and someone else's hunger.

Supporters of the Bush administration will lament its passing and opponents will rejoice. *The danger is that citizens will reject one path of empire without rejecting empire itself.* The deeper challenge is to build a sustainable republic. To do so, we need to understand and confront the religious roots of the U.S. Empire and the violent interpretations of Christianity that make it possible.

Notes

1. William Appleman Williams, *Empire as a Way of Life* (New York: Oxford University Press, 1980), ix.

2. Chalmers Johnson, *The Sorrows of Empire: Militarism, Secrecy, and the End of the Republic* (New York: Metropolitan Books, 2004), 8–9.

3. Chalmers Johnson, *Blowback: The Costs and Consequences of American Empire* (New York: Metropolitan Books, Henry Holt, 2000), 26.

4. Speech before the National Foreign Trade Convention, November 12, 1946.

5. *Congressional Record*, May 20, 1994, H3771.

6. Frank del Olmo, Editorial, *Los Angeles Times*, April 3, 1995.

7. Quoted in Michael T. Klare and Peter Kornbluth, eds., *Low Intensity Warfare: Counterinsurgency, Proinsurgency, and Antiterrorism in the Eighties* (New York: Pantheon Books, 1988), 48.

8. This quotation is taken from the written transcript of a Public Affairs Television special with Bill Moyers, entitled *The Secret Government: The Constitution in Crisis*. The program was a production of Alvin H. Perlmutter, Inc., and Public Affairs Television, Inc., in association with WNET and WETA. Copyright 1987 by Alvin H. Perlmutter, Inc., Public Affairs Television, Inc. The written transcript was produced by Journal Graphics, Inc., New York. Cf. Bill D. Moyers, *The Secret Government: The Constitution in Crisis: With Excerpts from "An Essay on Watergate"* (introduction, Henry Steele Commager; Cabin John, MD: Seven Locks, 1988; 2d ed., 1990).

9. Bob Woodward, *Veil: The Secret Wars of the C.I.A.* (New York: Simon & Schuster, 1987), 195, 173.

10. Quoted in William I. Robinson and Kent Norsworthy, *David and Goliath: The U.S. War against Nicaragua* (New York: Monthly Review, 1987), 26.

11. "Affidavit of Edgar Chamorro," Case Concerning Military and Paramilitary Activities in and against Nicaragua (*Nicaragua v. United States of America*), International Court of Justice, September 5, 1985, 17.

12. The CIA's Nicaraguan Manual: Joanne Omang and Aryeh Neier, *Psychological Operations in Guerrilla Warfare* (trans. of *Operaciones sicológicas en guerra de guerrillas*; New York: Random House, 1985), 33.

13. "Affidavit of Edgar Chamorro," 21.

14. Quoted in Leslie Cockburn, *Out of Control* (New York: Atlantic Monthly Press, 1987).

15. "Affidavit of Edgar Chamorro," 20–21.

16. Johnson, *Sorrows of Empire*, 11.

17. See Amnesty International USA, *Unmatched Power, Unmet Principles: The Human Rights Dimensions of US Training of Foreign Military and Police Forces* (New York: Amnesty International USA Publications, 2002), 1 (www.amnestyusa.org/stop torture/msp.pdf).

18. See UNICEF, *The State of the World's Children 1989* and *The State of the World's Children 1990* (New York: Oxford University Press, 1989–90).

19. Thomas L. Friedman, *The Lexus and the Olive Tree: Understanding Globalization* (New York: Farrar Straus Giroux, 1999), 8.

20. Ibid., 11.

21. Ibid., 350.

22. Ibid., 374, with emphasis added.

23. Mark Weisbrot, "Foreign Economic Policy," in *Power Trip: U.S. Unilateralism and Global Strategy after September 11* (ed. John Feffer; New York: Seven Stories, 2003), 86–87.

24. Friedman, *Lexus and the Olive Tree*, 17, with emphasis added.

25. Ibid., 212–13.

26. Ibid., 12, 197.

27. Ibid., 376.

28. Ibid., with emphasis in original.

29. Ibid., 373.

30. For a more detailed discussion of these costs, see Jack Nelson-Pallmeyer, *School of Assassins: Guns, Greed, and Globalization* (Maryknoll, NY: 2001), ch. 8.

31. Michael Mann, *Incoherent Empire* (London: Verso, 2003), 69, with emphasis added.

32. Ibid., 70.

33. Friedman, *Lexus and the Olive Tree,* 35, 273, 375, 373.

34. Ibid., 87, 88.

35. Ibid., 163.

36. Ibid., 161.

37. Ibid., 63.

38. Monte Hayes, "U.N.: Latin American Democracy in Trouble," www.philly-burbs.com/pb-dyn/news/88-04212004-286917.html.

39. Mann, *Incoherent Empire,* 75.

40. See Amnesty International, Annual Report, May 2004, http://web.amnesty.org/report2004/index-eng. See also Saul Landau, "Really Bad Trade News Obscured by Distractingly Bad News on Other Fronts," June 18, 2004, http://www.globalpolicy.org/socecon/trade/2004/0610liberalization.htm.

41. Paul Krugman, "Cronyism Part of What Went Wrong in Iraq," *Minneapolis Star Tribune,* June 30, 2004. For the single best article describing the disastrous economic agenda of the neoconservatives for a corporate dominated Iraq and how that agenda fueled the bloody insurgency, see Naomi Klein, "Baghdad Year Zero," *Harper's Magazgine,* September 2004.

42. William Hartung, *How Much Are You Making on the War, Daddy?* (New York: Nation Books, 2003), 4.

43. Johnson, *Sorrows of Empire,* 24.

44. Ibid., 4.

45. Ibid., 5.

46. Amnesty International USA, *Unmatched Power, Unmet Principles,* vii–viii.

47. Ibid., 255–56.

48. Emmanuel Todd, *After the Empire: The Breakdown of the American Order* (New York: Columbia University Press, 2002), 25.

6

BIBLICAL PERSPECTIVES ON VIOLENCE AND EMPIRE

Great harm has been done to us. We have suffered great loss. And in our grief and anger we have found our mission and our moment. Freedom and fear are at war. The advance of human freedom—the great achievement of our time, and the great hope of every time—now depends on us. . . . The course of this conflict is not known, yet its outcome is certain. Freedom and fear, justice and cruelty, have always been at war, and we know that God is not neutral between them.

—President George W. Bush[1]

Our encouragement and call to Muslims to enter Jihad against the American and the Israeli occupiers are actions which we are engaging in as religious obligations. Allah Most High has commanded us in many verses of the Qur'an to fight in His path and to urge the believers to do so. Of these are His words: "Fight in the path of Allah, you are not charged with the responsibility except for yourself, and urge the believers, lest Allah restrain the might of the rejectors, and Allah is stronger in might and stronger in inflicting punishment." . . . We have given an oath to Allah to continue in the struggle as long as we have blood pumping in our veins or a seeing eye, and we beg of Allah to accept and to grant a good ending for us and for all the Muslims.

—Osama bin Laden[2]

It seems almost as if there is something inherent in religious monotheism that lends itself to this kind of terrorist temptation. And our bland attempts to ignore this—to speak of this violence as if it did not have religious roots—is some kind of denial. We don't want to denigrate religion as such, and so we deny that religion is at the heart of this. But we would understand this conflict better, perhaps, if we first acknowledged that religion is responsible in some way, and then figure out how and why.

—Andrew Sullivan[3]

Crisis and Culpability

"There is no polite way to say that business is destroying the world." This is businessman Paul Hawken's blunt assessment of industry's role in the ecological crisis.[4] The poet Wendell Berry adds a corollary: "However destructive may be the policies of government and the methods and products of the corporation," the issue is "how we live. The world is being destroyed, no doubt about it—by the greed of the rich and powerful. It is also being destroyed by popular demand."[5] Their collective assessment of crisis and culpability applies equally well to U.S. Empire and the religious dynamics that make it possible.

There is no polite way to say that the U.S. Empire threatens the world and undermines the republic, and that it does so with the support or acquiescence of Christians. Although powerful corporate and government forces play leading roles, U.S. citizens tolerate or enable destructive empire. As a Christian, I am particularly concerned about Christian complicity. It is despicable that George Bush and Osama bin Laden use God and religion to justify brutal violence. Their willingness and success in doing so, however, both reflect and generate "popular demand."

There is growing concern about the relationship between religion and violence. In a December 2003 Minnesota Poll, "77 percent of respondents attributed at least a fair amount of the cause of the world's wars and conflict to religion."[6] Christians tend to see religion and violence as a problem for others and not themselves. Respondents to the Minnesota Poll focused almost exclusively on Islam. When "asked about specific religions, 34 percent said that Islam is more likely to encourage its believers to be violent, compared with 3 percent for Christianity, 5 percent for Judaism, 5 percent for Buddhism and 7 percent for Hinduism."[7]

The problem of Islam and violence demands attention.[8] The narrow focus on Islam, however, ignores what is arguably a graver problem. Many Christians who are concerned about Islam and violence seem unaware, unconcerned, or downright giddy that their "Christian nation" is the most militarized empire in world history. It is easy to see specks and logs in the eyes of others while collusion between Christianity and militarized empire goes unnoticed or is celebrated as God's will. The reality of violence at the heart of the U.S. Empire is buried beneath rhetorical avalanches with religious overtones that cover imperial ambitions.

In this chapter I explore the biblical roots of religious violence, including violent images of God that dominate the Bible and competing biblical themes concerning empire. Religiously justified violence generally, including its use to defend or oppose U.S. Empire, is not primarily the product of people misinterpreting or distorting "sacred" texts. It is rather a problem rooted in the actual violence at the heart of these texts that can be *reasonably cited* by people to justify their recourse to violence. This is "the elephant in the room of which nobody speaks."[9]

Justifying Violence

There are many reasons religion contributes to global bloodshed and Christianity enables or contributes to U.S. imperial violence. Religion deals with issues that believers associate with ultimate consequence and meaning. This makes religion important and dangerous, capable of inspiring compassion or violence. Religion can be used to justify violence and killing whenever conflicts are thought to intersect with issues of ultimate consequence. People rarely kill each other over religious differences alone, but they often use God to justify killing when conflicts escalate over other matters. In the midst of disputes over land, oppression, discrimination, or other historical grievances, violence is justified against others with subtle or not-so-subtle reference to "sacred" text, divine mission, or moral purpose. Attacking the U.S. Empire by killing Americans is a "religious obligation." Conversely, "as a blessed country" the United States is commissioned by God to build an empire in order to "rid the world of evil."

These abhorrent views mirror themes featured centrally in the Bible and the Quran. George Bush and Osama bin Laden understand faith, God, mission, and the nature of human and divine power in ways that are remarkably similar. This is not mere coincidence. The "sacred" texts of

Bush and bin Laden are dominated by violent images of God and violent interpretations of history, and they share a common rhetorical foundation of good versus evil.

The Bible and the Quran contain a rich reservoir of suspicion or hatred of the other that can be mined, refined, and used to justify violence. Dichotomies divide and distinguish: insiders or outsiders, good or evil, holy or profane, light or darkness, clean or unclean, blessed or cursed, heaven or hell, saved or condemned, God or Satan. To be an insider is to have been chosen and to choose wisely. Insiders are imbued with righteousness. They are bearers of sacred missions and potentially holy crusaders against infidels and other evildoers. Bruce Lincoln writes:

> Those who employ such discourses typically construe themselves as persons who understand and strive to realize God's will (or who strive to maintain the cosmic order, or at least to impose that order they define as rationale or progressive), while characterizing their opponents as religiously ignorant and/or rebellious. The effect is to cast those against whom they direct their violence as persons who need their direction and chastisement.[10]

The "sacred" texts of Jews, Christians, and Muslims speak of love and compassion but are dominated by images of a punishing, wrathful God. A scarcity of divine blessing fuels competition over limited rewards, reaching from Cain and Abel all the way to heaven. If you are an insider, God is wrathful toward others, but "God" loves you. Conversely, God is love, but "God" hates and punishes unrepentant sinners. God is just and hates injustice (however *you* define it), and neither you nor God can tolerate those who cause it. God is powerful but needs you whom "God" loves to execute justice on "God's" behalf against those whom "God" despises. When you and others whom God loves attack your enemies, your attack kills the enemies of God and thus fulfills a divine mission.

Religiously justified violence is the fruit of "sacred" texts that over-whelmingly privilege coercive understanding of power and images of a violent, punishing God. The Quran begins each sura (chapter) with com-forting words, "In the name of Allah, the Beneficent, the Merciful," but subsequent verses nearly always feature a wrathful, punishing God. There are threats of hell to discourage doubt or poor conduct or to motivate positive behavior; fear-generating stories nearly identical to their biblical counterparts, in which disobedience triggers God's punishing violence,

including plagues and floods; stories justifying human violence and warfare against religious others and enemies; promises of quick trips to Par-
adise for soldiers killed in battle; and accounts of God as holy warrior.[11]
The six pages of final instructions to the hijackers of September 11, 2001,
found in the luggage of Mohammed Atta, contained 89 references to God
and 22 quotations from the Quran.[12]

   The biblical God is also said to be compassionate but is most often
portrayed as a brutal killer and violent judge. God orders people to execute
children who curse their parents (Lev 20:1–2a, 9); sends forth she-bears to
maul children who insult a prophet (2 Kings 2:23–24); punishes disobedi-
ent people by reducing them to cannibalism (Lam 4:10–11); orders the
murder of all men, women and children after battle (Deut 20:16–17a;
Num 21:31–35); trades victory on the battlefield for a human blood sacrifice (Judg 11:30–39); drowns nearly all of creation and humanity in a punishing flood (Gen 6:13, 7:19–23); sends imperial armies to slaughter sinful
people (Isa 13:3, 5, 9, 15–17a); promises eternal punishment for those
who don't feed the hungry (Matt 25:41); demands human sacrifice,
recants, (Gen 22:2, 9b–12), and then uses the bloody sacrifice of Jesus to
atone for human sin (John 1:29); and promises to vindicate the faithful in
waves of end-time apocalyptic violence (Matt 3:7–8, 10, 12; Rev 11:17–18;
14:9–10).[13] Walter Wink writes:

> Biblical scholar Raymund Schwager points out that there are six
> hundred passages of explicit violence in the Hebrew Bible, one
> thousand verses where God's own violent actions of punishment are
> described, a hundred passages where Yahweh expressly commands
> others to kill people, and several stories where God irrationally kills
> or tries to kill for no apparent reason (for example, Exod. 4:24–26).
> Violence, Schwager concludes, is easily the most often mentioned
> activity in the Hebrew Bible.[14]

   Christians troubled by violence in the Old Testament tend to downplay
the many ways the New Testament writers reinforce violent images of
God. The Gospel writer known as Matthew, for example, frequently places
threatening and hateful words on the lips of Jesus. Matthew can't seem
to imagine people doing the right thing without violent threats hanging
over their heads. Feed the hungry or be sent "away into eternal punishment" (25:45–46).[15] Matthew's Jesus uses heavily apocalyptic imagery when
warning the people of the fiery judgment that is imminent:

Just as the weeds are collected and burned up with fire, so will it be at the end of the age. The Son of Man will send his angels, and they will collect out of his kingdom all causes of sin and all evildoers, and they will throw them into the furnace of fire, where there will be weeping and gnashing of teeth. (13:40–42)

Matthew positions characters in Jesus' parables as "God figures" that consistently send people to the torturers or to other terrible punishments. "Then the king said to the attendants, 'Bind him hand and foot, and throw him into the outer darkness, where there will be weeping and gnashing of teeth'" (22:13). Then "the master of that slave will come on a day when he does not expect him and at an hour that he does not know. He will cut him in pieces and put him with the hypocrites, where there will be weeping and gnashing of teeth" (24:50–51). "But his master replied, 'You wicked and lazy slave. . . . As for this worthless slave, throw him into the outer darkness, where there will be weeping and gnashing of teeth'" (25:26a, 30).

John the Baptist tells "the brood of vipers" who visit him in the wilderness that "every tree . . . that does not bear good fruit is cut down and thrown into the fire." The coming Messiah, with "his winnowing fork . . . in his hand, . . . will clear his threshing floor and will gather his wheat into his granary; but the chaff he will burn with unquenchable fire" (Matt 3:7–8, 10, 12). The book of Revelation warns:

Then the sixth angel blew his trumpet, and I heard a voice from the four horns of the golden altar before God, saying to the sixth angel who had the trumpet, "Release the four angels who are bound at the great river Euphrates." So the four angels were released, who had been held ready for the hour, the day, the month, and the year, to kill a third of humankind. (9:13–15)

The Gospel writers offer glimpses of a nonviolent stream linked to the historical Jesus, which challenges violent images of God and violent explanations of history. Unfortunately, it is marginalized within the New Testament, including by the Gospel writers themselves, and by most of subsequent Christianity. The marginalization of the nonviolent tradition linked to the historical Jesus has profound implications for how and why Christianity became the U.S. Empire's willing servant. I discuss this nonviolent stream in chapter 8. It offers compelling glimpses of a nonimperial Christianity more consistent with republic than empire.

"For the Bible Tells Me So"

If we say we do something because the Bible tells us to, then we should be required to name the places or passages in the Bible we consult for guidance as well as those we choose to ignore. Our course of action is likely to reflect our own biases and equally likely to be contradicted elsewhere in the Bible. God commands "Thou shall not kill" and yet orders and commits genocide. The Bible includes Jesus' teaching on love of enemies, but its primary definition of salvation is defeat of enemies. Jesus is presented as apocalyptic (announcing God's imminent violence to end the world) and nonapocalyptic. God is portrayed as pro-empire and anti-empire. In short, the Bible rarely agrees with itself. Incompatible and irreconcilable biblical perspectives on empire and other matters must be rejected altogether, or we must choose between them and explain our choices.

Biblical Story Lines

Competing biblical perspectives on empire can best be understood in the context of the violence of God traditions that dominate three major story lines of the Bible.[16] The first is the exodus, understood in the tradition as the story of *God's liberating violence.* Exodus theology said that God intervened in history on behalf of a chosen people who, although oppressed by the Egyptian Empire, was destined by God for greatness and freedom. With divine power God liberated the Israelites and ordered them to take control of a land occupied by others, a land within which to be God's people. God made a covenant with the chosen people that linked God's blessings to their faithfulness.

The second story line is exile, understood in the tradition as a story about *God's punishing violence.* Exile theology was born out of historical catastrophes. Exodus theology said the people of Israel were chosen by a powerful God and destined for freedom. Within real history over many hundreds of years, however, one empire after another dominated Israel (Assyrian, Babylonian, Persian, Seleucid, Roman). Exile theology explained the people's plight. They had displeased God, which triggered God's punishing violence. A classic statement of exile theology is found in Leviticus:

> If you follow my statutes and keep my commandments and observe them faithfully, I will give you your rains in their season, and the land shall yield its produce, and the trees of the field shall yield their

fruit. . . . And I will grant peace in the land, . . . and no sword shall go through your land. You shall give chase to your enemies, and they shall fall before you by the sword. . . . But if you will not obey me . . . and you break my covenant, I in turn will do this to you: I will bring terror on you; consumption and fever that waste the eyes and cause life to pine away. You shall sow your seed in vain, for your enemies shall eat it. I will set my face against you, and you shall be struck down by your enemies; your foes shall rule over you, and you shall flee though no one pursues you. And if in spite of this you will not obey me, I will continue to punish you sevenfold for your sins. . . . I will bring the sword against you, executing vengeance for the covenant; and if you withdraw within our cities, I will send pestilence among you, and you shall be delivered into enemy hands. . . . You shall eat the flesh of your sons, and you shall eat the flesh of your daughters. I will destroy your high places and cut down your incense altars; I will heap your carcasses on the carcasses of your idols. I will abhor you. I will lay your cities waste, will make your sanctuaries desolate, and I will not smell your pleasing odors. I will devastate the land, so that your enemies who come to settle in it shall be appalled at it. And you I will scatter among the nations, and I will unsheathe the sword against you; your land shall be a desolation, and your cities a waste. (26:3–7, 14–18, 25–33)

Exile theology focused on God's punishing violence, but it often included the promise of a glorious reversal in fortune. God's violence, although deserved, was temporary. The people could trigger God's liberating violence through proper conduct and correct worship. Israel would then be restored to greatness.

The third main biblical story line promised *God's vindicating violence* at the end of history. Like exile theology, apocalyptic theology responded to historical disappointments and calamities. The glorious reversal promised by the theologians of exile did not materialize, and oppression intensified at the hands of foreign rulers. As a result, apocalyptic theology was and is extremely pessimistic about history: Earthly existence is hopelessly corrupt and human beings cannot do much to improve things. God is fighting a cosmic battle between good and evil and is thus preoccupied and unable to redeem Israel. The good news is that God will soon win a final cosmic battle against evil. God will rule and eventually end the world, punish evildoers, and vindicate the faithful with resurrection and a permanent, heavenly reward. The payoff for fidelity would include the satisfaction of having their enemies fry. According to the apocalyptic book of Daniel:

> At that time Michael, the great prince, the protector of your people, shall arise. There shall be a time of anguish, such as has never occurred since nations first came into existence. But at that time your people shall be delivered, everyone who is found written in the book. Many of those who sleep in the dust of the earth shall awake, some to everlasting life, and some to shame and everlasting contempt. Those who are wise shall shine like the brightness of the sky, and those who lead many to righteousness, like the stars forever and ever. (Dan 12:1–3)

The New Testament writers interpret Jesus in an apocalyptic light. For example, Mark's Jesus says:

> Then they will see "the Son of Man coming in clouds" with great power and glory. Then he will send out the angels, and gather his elect from the four winds, from the ends of the earth to the ends of heaven. . . . Truly I tell you, this generation will not pass away until all these things have taken place. (Mark 13:26–27, 30)

A Pro-Empire Stream

The Bible has a pro-empire stream, an anti-imperial stream linked to God's violence, and a nonviolent anti-imperial stream rooted in the historical Jesus. The first two are discussed here, and the third in chapter 8.

God's promise to Abraham is that he will be the father of empire, "a great and mighty nation" (Gen 18:18). In response to Abraham's willingness to kill his son Isaac, God says: "I will indeed bless you, and I will make your offspring as numerous as the stars of heaven and as the sand that is on the seashore. And your offspring will possess the gate of their enemies" (22: 17).

The biblical hero Joseph has a cozy relationship with the Egyptian Empire and is blessed by God. God made Joseph "a father to Pharaoh, and lord of all his house and ruler over all the land of Egypt" (Gen 45:8). Although the Exodus story is said to express God's commitment to liberate oppressed people from empire, there is no sign of God being averse to empire in the Joseph accounts. God blesses Joseph, who rules the Egyptian

Empire on behalf of Pharaoh. Joseph's father (Jacob) blesses Pharaoh. Pharaoh in turn allows Jacob and Joseph's brothers to settle "in the land of Egypt, in the best part of the land" (47:11).

No human or divine character in the story is the least bit hostile to empire. All benefit from and have a role in imperial power. Joseph pleases both God and Pharaoh and pleases God by serving Pharaoh. With God's blessing he enriches the Pharaoh and dramatically expands the power of the Egyptian Empire. Joseph uses food as a weapon against both Israelites and Egyptians in ways that would have made any IMF structural adjustment broker proud. Imagine Joseph in a business suit of many colors.

Step 1 is to get all the money:

Now there was no food in all the land, for the famine was very severe. The land of Egypt and the land of Canaan languished because of the famine. Joseph collected all the money to be found in the land of Egypt and the land of Canaan, in exchange for the grain that they bought; and Joseph brought the money into Pharaoh's house. (47:14)

Step 2 is to take control of all the livestock:

When the money from the land of Egypt and from the land of Canaan was spent, all the Egyptians came to Joseph, and said, "Give us food! Why should we die before your eyes? For our money is gone." And Joseph answered, "Give me your livestock, and I will give you food in exchange for your livestock, if your money is gone." So they brought their livestock to Joseph; and Joseph gave them food in exchange for the horses, the flocks, the herds, and the donkeys. That year he supplied them with food in exchange for all their livestock. (47:15–17)

Step 3 is to enslave all Egyptians and take their land:

When that year was ended, they came to him the following year, and said to him, "We can not hide from my lord that our money is all spent; and the herds of cattle are my lord's. There is nothing left in the sight of my lord but our bodies and our lands. Shall we die before your eyes, both we and our land? Buy us and our land in exchange for food. We with our land will become slaves to Pharaoh;

just give us seed, so that we may live and not die, and that the land may not become desolate." So Joseph bought all the land of Egypt for Pharaoh. All the Egyptians sold their fields, because the famine was severe upon them; and the land became Pharaoh's. As for the people, he made slaves of them from one end of Egypt to the other. (47:18–21)

The book of Exodus picks up the story after Joseph's use of food as a weapon on behalf of Pharaoh. It begins with a report that "the Israelites were fruitful and prolific; they multiplied and grew exceedingly strong, so that the land [Egypt] was filled with them" (1:7). The story begins, in other words, not with a portrait of vulnerable Israelites but rather with a privileged, prolific, and powerful people, poised to take over a land that is not their own.

Prophetic promises offer a final example of a pro-empire perspective within the Bible. Exile theology promises were at times manifestly imperial:

Thus says the LORD God: I will soon lift up my hand to the nations, and raise my signal to the peoples; and they shall bring your sons in their bosom, and your daughters shall be carried on their shoulders. Kings shall be your foster fathers, and their queens your nursing mothers. With their faces to the ground they shall bow down to you, and lick the dust off your feet. Then you will know that I am the LORD; those who wait for me shall not be put to shame. . . . I will contend with those who contend with you, and I will save your children. I will make your oppressors eat their own flesh, and they shall be drunk with their own blood as with wine. Then all flesh shall know that I am the LORD your Savior, and your Redeemer, the Mighty One of Jacob. (Isa 49:22–23, 25b–26)

Foreigners shall build up your walls, and their kings shall minister to you; for in my wrath I struck you down, but in my favor I have had mercy on you. Your gates shall always be open; day and night they shall not be shut, so that nations shall bring you their wealth, with their kings led in procession. For the nation and kingdom that will not serve you shall perish; those nations shall be utterly laid waste. (60:10–12).

Isaiah promises empire, including sweet victory and sweet revenge. The oppressed one day would be oppressors within God's Empire. Enemies would bow down and lick the dust from the people's feet: "The house of Israel will possess the nations as male and female slaves in the LORD's land; they will take captive those who were their captors, and rule over those who oppressed them" (14:1–2).

An Anti-imperial Stream

The most prominent biblical perspective on empire is an anti-imperial stream linked to divine and/or human violence. This stream dominates the tradition because although many of the biblical writers aspired to empire, history dealt them a bad hand. Foreign domination was so widespread and brutal that it fed biblical theologies of holy war, messianic desires, hate-filled fantasies of apocalyptic violence, and more than a little schizophrenia. Schizophrenia resulted not only because there were both pro- and anti-imperial theologies, but also because exile theology embraced the idea that God used foreign empires to punish the people, but one day would crush these empires and free Israel:

> Ah, Assyria, the rod of my anger—the club in their hands is my fury! Against a godless nation I send him, and against the people of my wrath I command him, to take spoil and seize plunder, and to tread them down like the mire of the streets. (Isa 10:5–6)

> When the Lord has finished all his work on Mount Zion and on Jerusalem, he will punish the arrogant boasting of the king of Assyria and his haughty pride. . . . Therefore the Sovereign, the LORD of hosts, will send wasting sickness among his stout warriors, and under his glory a burning will be kindled, like the burning of fire. (10:12, 16)

The Bible's anti-imperial stream is rooted in promises and expectations of God's violence. According to Exodus theology, a holy warrior-God liberated slaves from the Egyptian Empire. "The LORD is a warrior; the LORD is his name. Pharaoh's chariots and his army he cast into the sea; his picked officers were sunk in the Red Sea" (Exod 15:3–4).

> Moses said, "Thus says the LORD: About midnight I will go out through Egypt. Every firstborn in the land of Egypt shall die, from the firstborn of Pharaoh who sits on his throne to the firstborn of

the female slave who is behind the handmill, and all the firstborn of the livestock. Then there will be a loud cry throughout the whole land of Egypt, such as has never been or will ever be again." (Exod 11:4–6)

Troubling features abound within this anti-imperial "liberation" story and subsequent conquest of the "promised land." The Exodus story establishes divine and human violence as keys to "justice," and it legitimizes genocide. For "I will hand over to you the inhabitants of the land, and you shall drive them out before you" (Exod 23:31b). "You must utterly destroy them. . . . Show them no mercy" (Deut 7:2). "For it was the LORD's doing to harden their hearts so that they would come against Israel in battle, in order that they might be utterly destroyed, and might receive no mercy, but be exterminated, just as the LORD had commanded" (Josh 11:20).

The Exodus story also equates power with violence and establishes *superior violence* as the proper measure of divinity. God proves to be God among competing claimants through superior violence:

Has any god ever attempted to go and take a nation for himself from the midst of another nation, by trials, by signs and wonders, by war, by a mighty hand and an outstretched arm, and by terrifying displays of power, as the LORD your God did for you in Egypt before your very eyes? To you it was shown so that you would acknowledge that the LORD is God; there is no other besides him. (Deut 4:34–35)

It is God's superior violence that inspires belief, allegiance, and worship:

For the LORD will pass through to strike down the Egyptians; when he sees the blood on the lintel and on the two doorposts, the LORD will pass over that door and will not allow the destroyer to enter your houses to strike you down. You shall observe this rite as a perpetual ordinance for you and your children. When you come to the land that the LORD will give you, as he has promised, you shall keep this observance. And when your children ask you, "What do you mean by this observance?" you shall say, "It is the Passover sacrifice to the LORD, for he passed over the houses of the Israelites in Egypt, when he struck down the Egyptians but spared our houses." And the people bowed down and worshiped. (Exod 12:23–27)

The Exodus story also establishes the meaning of salvation as defeat of enemies, a definition that came to dominate the Bible:

Thus the LORD *saved* Israel that day from the Egyptians; and Israel saw the Egyptians dead on the seashore. (Exod 14:30, emphasis added)

Foreigners lost heart, and came trembling out of their strongholds. The LORD lives! Blessed be my rock, and exalted be the God of *my salvation,* the God who gave me vengeance and subdued peoples under me; who delivered me from my enemies. (Ps 18:45–48a, emphasis added)

It will be said on that day, Lo, this is our God; we have waited for him, so that he might *save* us. This is the LORD for whom we have waited; let us be glad and rejoice in his *salvation.* For the hand of the LORD will rest on this mountain. The Moabites shall be trodden down in their place as straw is trodden down in a dung-pit. (Isa 25:9–10, emphasis added)

The biblical writers thus portray God as powerful and capable of liberating the people, but the people themselves were subjugated and dominated by foreign empires. Although there was no agreement about why this happened or what the people should do differently, nearly all Jews living in first-century Palestine embraced one of two anti-imperial scenarios by which empire would be judged or defeated. Some expected God to send a military Messiah, who would help them defeat their enemies (now Roman) and bring Israel to prominence. According to this view, human violence was part of an anti-imperial struggle that would be aided by God.

Others became disillusioned with messianic promises. History had taught them that redemption (salvation) was impossible within history, and so they embraced apocalyptic expectations. God would come soon to end history as we know it, defeat evil, destroy destructive empires, and vindicate the faithful. According to this view, human violence wasn't a necessary part of the anti-imperial struggle. The people could wait, prepare, or act nonviolently with confidence that God's apocalyptic violence would bring an end to empire at the end of human history.

Then another angel, a third, followed them, crying with a loud voice, "Those who worship the beast and its image, and receive a mark on their foreheads or on their hands, they will also drink the wine of God's wrath, poured unmixed into the cup of his anger, and they will be tormented with fire and sulfur in the presence of the holy angels and in the presence of the Lamb." (Rev 14:9–10)

Christian support for U.S. Empire is grounded in many of the violent images of God and expectations of history discussed above. Chapter 7 explores this convergence. Chapter 8 examines the nonviolent anti-imperial stream associated with Jesus and its relevance for those of us who are committed to helping the United States transition from empire to republic, and committed to helping Christianity break its ties to brutal empire and its addiction to violence.

Notes

1. "President's Remarks to the Nation," September 11, 2002.
2. Emergency Net NEWS Service, 1998, http://www.emergency.com/bladen98.htm.
3. Andrew Sullivan, "This *Is* a Religious War," *New York Times Magazine*, October 7, 2001, 45–46.
4. Paul Hawken, *The Ecology of Commerce* (New York: Harper Business, 1993).
5. Ibid., 14–15.
6. Martha Sawyer Allen, "Religion Seen as Significant Factor in War," *Minneapolis Star Tribune* (December 28, 2003).
7. Sawyer Allen, "Religion Seen as Significant Factor in War."
8. See Jack Nelson-Pallmeyer, *Is Religion Killing Us? Violence in the Bible and the Quran* (Harrisburg, PA: Trinity Press International, 2003). There I describe violence of God traditions at the heart of the Bible and the Quran, including many dozens of passages from the Quran that could be reasonably interpreted to justify violence in defense of faith or in pursuit of justice; especially see ch. 6. For an unusually candid critique of Islam and violence by a Muslim, see Irshad Manji, *The Trouble with Islam: A Muslim's Call for Reform in Her Faith* (New York: St. Martin's Press, 2003).
9. Nelson-Pallmeyer, *Is Religion Killing Us?* xiv–xv.
10. Bruce Lincoln, *Holy Terrors: Thinking about Religion after September 11* (Chicago: Chicago University Press, 2003), 34.
11. For a detailed look at violence in the Quran, including numerous citations from the Quran itself, see Nelson-Pallmeyer, *Is Religion Killing Us?* ch. 6.
12. Lincoln, *Holy Terrors*, 11–12.
13. For a detailed look at violence in the Bible, see Jack Nelson-Pallmeyer, *Jesus against Christianity: Reclaiming the Missing Jesus* (Harrisburg, PA: Trinity Press International, 2001), chs. 3–5.
14. Walter Wink, *The Powers That Be: Theology for A New Millennium* (New York: Doubleday, 1998), 84–85.

15. Except as otherwise indicated, citations of the Hebrew Bible and Christian New Testament are from the NRSV (1989): Michael D. Coogan et al., eds., *The New Oxford Annotated Bible: New Revised Standard Version with the Apocrypha* (3d ed.; New York: Oxford University Press, 2001); online NRSV, http://www.devotions.net/bible/00bible.htm. See also Warren Carter, *Matthew and Empire: Initial Explorations* (Harrisburg, PA: Trinity Press International, 2001).

16. See Nelson-Pallmeyer, *Jesus against Christianity,* chs. 7–10.

CHRISTIANITY IN SERVICE TO EMPIRE

[When Bush said,] "These are God-given values. These aren't United States values," . . . [the] implication was clear: To spread American values was to be on the side of God, to resist them was to oppose God.

—Claes G. Ryn[1]

[The Bush administration's] grand strategy may prove more radically disruptive of world order than anything the terrorists of September 11, 2001, could have hoped to achieve on their own. Through its actions, the United States seems determined to bring about precisely the threats that it says it is trying to prevent. Its apparent acceptance of a "clash of civilizations" and of wars to establish moral truth that is the same in every culture sounds remarkably like a jihad, especially given the Bush administration's ties to Christian fundamentalism.

—Chalmers Johnson[2]

The dominant values of American life—affluence, achievement, appearance, power, competition, consumption, individualism—are vastly different from anything recognizably Christian. As individuals and as a culture our existence has become massively idolatrous.

—Marcus Borg[3]

Deep Roots

It is tempting to deny the breadth and depth of U.S. imperial history and to believe that the U.S. Empire began and will end with the Bush administration. It is also tempting to believe that the problem of Christianity and empire is limited to the extremist views of legalistic Christians that made up the strongest block of Bush supporters. When I highlight the need to resist these temptations, I do not mean to take attention from the monumental dangers posed by the Bush administration's grand strategy for militarized empire and the theocratic and oftentimes bizarre religious views of his supporters. Minimizing these dangers would be fundamentally irresponsible. Christian support for empire, like the problem of empire itself, however, has deeper roots and broader implications.

Bizarre and Dangerous

The Bible is a useful book for U.S. leaders committed to empire and eager to construct religious justifications for their ambitions. Its pages and those who find inspiration in them offer a smorgasbord of potential building blocks for empire. Pillars can be constructed with bizarre materials taken from the stockpiles of conservative, legalistic, and fundamentalist-leaning Christians. They include apocalyptic fantasies, wrathful views of God, suspicion and fear of others, literal interpretations, preoccupations with heaven and hell, myths of Armageddon, and expectations of the rapture. Bruce Bawer's description of legalistic Christianity's threat to U.S democracy sheds light on theocratic dangers at the heart of the Bush administration's broader imperial project, including its grand strategy for global domination cast as a permanent war to rid the world of evil:

> The problem with legalistic Christianity is not simply that it affirms that God can be evil; it's that it imagines a manifestly evil God and calls that evil good. In effect, . . . *it worships evil*. In America right now, millions of children are taught by their legalistic Christian parents and ministers to revere a God of wrath and to take a sanguine view of human suffering. They are taught to view their fellow Americans not as having been "created equal," as the Declaration of Independence would have it, but as being saved or unsaved, children of God or creatures of Satan; they are taught not to respect those most different from themselves but to regard them as the enemy, to

resist their influence, and to seek to restrict their rights. This is not only morally offensive, it's socially dangerous—and it represents . . . a very real menace to democratic civil society.[4]

The menace posed by legalistic Christians stretches to the whole world, but they don't have to *imagine* a manifestly evil God to justify their views and actions. It is more accurate to say that they privilege wrathful images over others when they read the Bible, shape their faith, or seek to shape domestic and foreign policies. At the heart of their theology is a presumed scarcity of divine blessing that fosters competition over limited earthly and heavenly rewards. They paint the world as a politically and spiritually dangerous place in which enemies, or even people with whom they differ, are to be feared and defeated. Regrettably, their views on God's wrath and the scarcity of divine blessing rest on *solid theological ground.*

The same can be said of legalistic Christianity's despicable explanation for the terrorist attacks of September 11, 2001. Two days after the attack, Jerry Falwell and Pat Robertson claimed that an angry God had allowed the terrorists to succeed. Falwell told Robertson on the *700 Club*: "What we saw on Tuesday, as terrible as it is, could be miniscule if, in fact, God continues to lift the curtain and allow the enemies of America to give us probably what we deserve." Robertson responded, "Jerry, that's my feeling. I think we've just seen the antechamber to terror. We haven't even begun to see what they can do to the major population." On the same program Falwell said: "The abortionists have got to bear some burden for this because God will not be mocked. And when we destroy 40 million little innocent babies, we make God mad. I really believe that the pagans, and the abortionists, and the feminists, and the gays and the lesbians who are actively trying to make that an alternative lifestyle, the A.C.L.U., People for the American Way, all of them who have tried to secularize America, I point the finger in their face and say, 'You helped this happen.'" To which Robertson responded: "Well, I totally concur, and the problem is we have adopted that agenda at the highest levels of government." Robertson also issued a press release in which he said that "God almighty is lifting his protection from us" because our country is rampant with materialism, Internet pornography, and lack of prayer.[5] Bush himself indicated his support for this theology when he declared on the *700 Club*:

The prayer that I would like America to ask for is to pray for God's protection for our land and for our people. . . . [To pray] that there's a *shield of protection,* so that if the evil ones try to hit us again, that we've done everything we can, physically, and that there is *a spiritual shield that protects the country.*[6]

This interpretation of 9/11 should make it clear that post-9/11 holy wars against evil have both domestic and foreign targets. Falwell and Robertson were widely and rightfully condemned for their explanation of 9/11 in the secular press and by mainstream Christians. Lamentably, however, many believed them because they are faithful to one of the Bible's most dominant themes: God's punishing violence. There are hundreds of biblical passages similar to these:

Ah, you who call evil good and good evil, who put darkness for light and light for darkness, who put bitter for sweet and sweet for bitter! . . . Therefore the anger of the LORD was kindled against his people, and he stretched out his hand against them and struck them; the mountains quaked, and their corpses were like refuse in the streets. (Isa 5: 20, 25)

Then Jeremiah said to them: "Thus you shall say to Zedekiah: Thus says the LORD, the God of Israel: I am going to turn back the weapons of war that are in your hands and with which you are fighting against the king of Babylon and against the Chaldeans who are besieging you outside the walls; and I will bring them together into the center of this city. I myself will fight against you with out-stretched hand and mighty arm, in anger, in fury, and in great wrath. And I will strike down the inhabitants of this city, both human beings and animals; they shall die of a great pestilence." (Jer 21:3–6)

See, the day of the LORD comes, cruel, with wrath and fierce anger, to make the earth a desolation, and to destroy its sinners from it. . . . Whoever is found will be thrust through, and whoever is caught will fall by the sword. Their infants will be dashed to pieces before their eyes; their houses will be plundered, and their wives ravished. See, I am stirring up the Medes against them. (Isa 13:9, 15–17a; cf. 13:3).

Legalistic Christians wholeheartedly embrace this theology and these violent images of God. As a matter of faith, they supported Bush and theocracy at home, and a crusade against evil abroad. Religion, as Kevin

Phillips wrote, had been a "critical engine for a Bush triumph" in the 2000 presidential election:

> Perhaps because of how this tide of moral outrage [in response to revelation of Clinton's moral turpitude] had come to arouse southern fundamentalist constituencies, George W. Bush began to emphasize and display unusual personal religiosity. He cast himself as the prodigal son, brought back to God after waywardness and crisis. From 1994 to 2000, he repeatedly used such biblically inflected language about good and evil that one could almost hear the words of Daniel and Jeremiah. So close did he draw to evangelical and fundamentalist Protestant leaders that in 2001, the *Washington Post* suggested that the new president had virtually replaced evangelist Pat Robertson as the leader of the U.S. Religious Right.[7]

Most legalistic Christians believe the world is rapidly approaching a cataclysmic end, in which they will triumph and others will be condemned. Kevin Phillips wrote: "The fact that almost half of U.S. Christians believed in Armageddon—a striking anomaly in the Western world—was enough to chill even a brave Washington legislator." "More than seven of every ten Texans believe that the Bible is God's word and that all its prophecies will transpire." In the 2000 election, "roughly 55 percent of Bush voters were Armageddon believers."[8]

End-time theologies are rooted in bizarre apocalyptic fantasies involving what Bawer calls "a free interpretation of the extremely obscure symbolic account of the Apocalypse in the Book of Revelation."[9] They envision Jesus quite literally dropping from the sky and meeting true-to-Christ Christians in the air (known as the rapture). At this time all the faithful who had died throughout prior history will rise and join together with the living generation of believers to live with Jesus. The rapture will be followed by numerous tribulations, including God's vengeance against faithless nations, a monumental battle in which Christ defends Jerusalem from Satan, and judgment of the Jews who reject Jesus. Jesus will destroy all his enemies. Some groups envision a thousand-year period in which Jesus rules the earth. All embrace the idea that Jesus will oversee a final judgment, in which Satan and all unbelievers will be cast into a lake of fire and burn forever.[10]

A popularized view of the coming apocalypse is provided in the novel *Glorious Appearing*. "Writers and artists have been imagining the Second

Coming of Jesus for 2,000 years," David Kirkpatrick writes, "but few have portrayed him wreaking more carnage on the unbelieving world than [the authors] Tim LaHaye and Jerry B. Jenkins." "Their Jesus appears from the clouds on a white horse with a 'conviction like a flame of fire' in his eyes. With all the gruesome detail of a Hollywood horror movie, Jesus eviscerates the flesh of millions of unbelievers merely by speaking." Kirkpatrick offers glimpses into the novel's content as well as its political significance:

> "Men and women soldiers and horses seemed to explode where they stood," Dr. LaHaye and Mr. Jenkins write. "It was as if the very words of the Lord had superheated their blood, causing it to burst through their veins and skin." The authors add, "Even as they struggled, their own flesh dissolved, their eyes melted and their tongues disintegrated."
>
> Dr. LaHaye and Mr. Jenkins did not invent fire and brimstone. But some scholars who study religion say that the phenomenal popularity of their "Left Behind" series of apocalyptic thrillers—now the best-selling adult novels in the United States—are part of a shift in American culture's image of Jesus. The gentle, pacifist Jesus of the Crucifixion is sharing the spotlight with a more muscular warrior Jesus of the Second Coming, the Lamb making way for the Lion.
>
> Scholars . . . say the trend partly reflects the growing clout of evangelical Christians and the relative decline of the liberal mainline Protestant denominations over the last 30 years. The image of a fearsome Jesus who will turn the tables on the unbelieving earthly authorities corresponds to a widespread sense among many conservative Christians that their values are under assault in a culture war with the secular society around them. The shift coincides with a surging interest in Biblical prophecies of the apocalypse around the turn of the millennium, the terrorist attacks of Sept. 11 and the two wars with Iraq. And the warlike image of Jesus also fits with President George W. Bush's discussions of a godly purpose behind American military actions in Afghanistan and Iraq.[11]

Some legalistic Christians embrace a Dominion theology, which calls on the people of God to seize earthly power in an effort to create conditions ripe for Armageddon. Kevin Phillips has described their motivation: "Prayer and evangelism were not enough; a Christian-led political and social reformation was necessary because Christ will not return to earth until a revived church has set the scene." "A president convinced that God was speaking to him . . . might through Dominionism start to view himself as an agent called by the Almighty to restore the earth to godly control."[12] This sheds light on President Bush's statement to Palestinian Prime Minister Mahmoud Abbas: "God told me to strike al-Qaida and I struck them, and then he instructed me to strike at Saddam, which I did, and now I am determined to solve the problem in the Middle East. If you help me I will act, and if not, the elections will come and I will have to focus on them."

Bruce Lincoln has observed that President Bush's political discourse often contains biblical allusions or subtexts:

> These allusions provide a thunderous moral condemnation running parallel to Bush's more prosaic characterizations of the enemy as outlaws, murderers, criminals, and terrorists. The biblical subtext is not redundant, however. Rather, for those who have ears to hear, these allusions effect a qualitative transformation, giving Bush's message an entirely different status. This conversion of secular political speech into religious discourse invests otherwise merely human events with transcendent significance. By the end, America's adversaries have been redefined as enemies of God, and current events have been constituted as confirmation of Scripture.[13]

Legalistic or fundamentalistic theologies are widespread and politically dangerous because they are intractable. As William Ray says, "Fundamentalism demands believers, not thinkers." There is "no evidence, no logic, no personal experience, *nothing* can change the fundamentalist's mind about 'revealed truth.'"[14] One observer, whose "entire family is born-again" and "completely focused" on "Armageddon and The Rapture," stated: "Most fundamentalist readers I know accept the [Left Behind] series as an absolute reality soon coming to a godless planet near you. It helps to understand that everything is literal in the Fundamentalist voter universe." He added, "Just because millions of Christians appear to be dangerously nuts does not mean they are marginal."[15]

The Fundamentalism Project of the American Academy of Arts and Sciences identified common characteristics of fundamentalists within a variety of religious traditions. It found "a discernible pattern of religious militance by which self-styled 'true believers' attempt to arrest the erosion of religious identity, fortify the borders of the religious community, and create viable alternatives to secular institutions and behaviors."[16] "In the United States after 9/11," Phillips observed, "only Muslim fanatics and religious extremists were generally so identified. U.S. citizens working to bring on Armageddon were not."[17]

The Bush administration's grand strategy for U.S. Empire based on permanent military superiority needs to be understood in basic continuity with the past. It marked, as I mentioned earlier, an extreme point but rested squarely on rather than apart from a continuum tracking U.S. foreign policies in service to empire. Legalistic Christianity's theology must be similarly understood. Its violent images of God and expectations of history unabashedly served militarized empire. It too, however, rested and rests on a continuum with many other violent theologies and other Christian expressions that are generally supportive of U.S. Empire.

Unlikely Servant

Christianity was a bizarre candidate to become a servant of militarized empire. It was born in the context of an anti-imperial people with a long tradition of hostility to empire. Jews in first-century Palestine resented injustices and indignities connected to foreign occupation and longed for freedom from Rome. The cross was Rome's preferred instrument of state terror; Jesus, a founder of an anti-Roman Jewish reform movement, was crucified by the empire with support from collaborating members of the Jewish aristocracy and priestly elites.[18] Jesus resisted Roman arrogance and power but through nonviolent means. He taught love of enemies, advocated and practiced nonviolence, and warned that using violence led to more violence.

An anti-imperial thrust was also visible in the early church. Christians declared "Christ is Lord" in direct opposition to Roman imperial claims concerning the emperor. About forty years before Jesus' birth, the Roman Senate declared the emperor Julius Caesar divine. His son, Octavius, was the "son of a divine one." His birth was heralded as "the beginning of the good news." Octavius was known as a savior who brought peace to the world through war.[19] The first verse of Mark's Gospel offers an anti-imperial counter claim: "The beginning of the good news of Jesus Christ, the Son of God" (1:1). If you want to know where God is working in history, then look not to empire, Mark said, but to a victim of empire, the crucified nobody named Jesus. Paul established his alternative Christian communities precisely where the Roman emperor cult and imperial patronage system were strongest. Christian communities, in other words, were established in direct opposition with and as fledgling alternatives to the Roman imperial system.[20]

When Christianity took on a radical apocalyptic edge, it did so out of frustration with the arrogant, abusive, and enduring power of the Roman Empire. Rome was the target of its violent fantasies. Unable to defeat Rome in history, apocalyptic Christianity warned Christians not to be seduced by Roman power. It imagined the defeat of the Roman Empire and Christianity's own vindication through God's apocalyptic violence at the end time. According to the book of Revelation:

> "We give you thanks, Lord God Almighty, who are and who were, for you have taken your great power and begun to reign. The nations raged, but your wrath has come, and the time for judging the dead, for rewarding your servants, the prophets and saints and all who fear your name, both small and great, and for destroying those who destroy the earth." (11:17–18)
>
> Then another angel, a third, followed them, crying with a loud voice, "Those who worship the beast and its image, and receive a mark on their foreheads or on their hands, they will also drink the wine of God's wrath, poured unmixed into the cup of his anger, and they will be tormented with fire and sulfur in the presence of the holy angels and in the presence of the Lamb." (14:10)
>
> "Therefore her plagues will come in a single day—pestilence and mourning and famine—and she will be burned with fire; for mighty is the Lord God who judges her." (18:8)

Although the Gospel writers interpreted Jesus in an apocalyptic light, the early church's commitment to Jesus' nonviolence lasted almost three hundred years. "It is noteworthy," John Driver wrote in *How Christians Made Peace with War*, "that between 100 and 313 no Christian writers, to our knowledge, approved of Christian participation in warfare." According to Driver:

> The objections of early Christians to warfare and military service were based in the teachings and example of Jesus. This led them to resist stubbornly the evils and the injustices of their time. But in doing this, they resolutely refused to respond to evildoers with violence. They were even willing to suffer persecution and death

rather than to shed blood of their persecutors. Respecting the lives of their enemies, they refused to contribute to the vicious spiral of violence.[21]

The "emperor's godlike nature was a political matter" for Christians. "Emperors officially proclaimed themselves gods and sons of gods." The army "required an oath of loyalty to the emperor-gods," which Christians who acknowledged the lordship of Christ felt compelled to refuse. The church father Tertullian also recognized the contradiction between the vocation of a soldier and the example of Jesus:

> Shall it be held lawful to make an occupation of the sword, when the Lord proclaims that he who uses the sword shall perish by the sword? And shall the son of peace take part in the battle when it does not become him even to sue at law? And shall he apply the chain, and the prison, and the torture, and the punishment, who is not the avenger even of his own wrongs?[22]

This strong, nonviolent, anti-imperial stream ended in 313 with Emperor Constantine's edict of toleration, which paved the way for Christianity to become the official religion of the Roman Empire. "His order marked a new era for the Christian church's attitude toward military service. From then on," Driver says, "Christians began to serve actively in the military in obedience to the state."[23]

Useful Themes

It took hundreds of years for Christianity to move from being a non-violent, minority religion persecuted by empire to being a violent, official religion of the Roman Empire. Nonviolence eventually gave way to just war as the church sold its soul in exchange for a seat at the table with the powerful. Jesus Christ replaced Mithras, the Roman God and guardian of Roman troops, and took over his birthday, December 25. The rejection of nonviolence and embrace of a pro-imperial trajectory led dominant Christianity to become the servant of violent empire, eventually including U.S. Empire. This mutation is not as strange as it may seem.

The Bible offers competing portraits and stories about God, faith, and historical destiny from which to choose, including a pro- and an anti-imperial stream. That is why today we can have liberation theology

Christians in Latin America and imperial Christians in the United States, all living under the same tent, even though they are diametrically opposed on almost every religious and political issue. They read the same Bible from radically different historical vantage points, picking and choosing verses, stories, and themes along the way. Ironically, one of the few things they share from their readings of the Bible is the presumption that God's violence is on their side. More ironic still, biblically speaking they both are arguably right.

Dominant Christianity's transition from being persecuted to privileged and powerful is another example of theology adapting to historical circumstances. Aspirations to empire rooted in God's will, favor, and power were part of the tradition from the very beginning. Dire historical circumstances prevented their realization. This gave rise to exodus theology's longing for liberation, exile theology's explanation for historical catastrophes and promise of glorious reversals, and to apocalyptic theology's despair about history altogether and its projection of end-time vindication through unimaginable divine violence.

Many biblical themes discussed in chapter 6 were adapted and reached ascendancy in the context of U.S. Empire. All Christianity had to do to become a servant to the U.S. Empire was to stress certain biblical themes over others and to interpret and apply them on behalf of imperial objectives. The Bible offers a rich and deep reservoir of diverse and incompatible ideas about God and faith from which to choose. Useful themes adaptable to U.S. Empire include the idea of a particular people being chosen by God; the notion that God works through an exceptional nation to accomplish divine purposes; the association of salvation with defeat of enemies; the definition of divine and human power as superior violence; the belief that historical prominence is a sign of God's blessing; and the use of sharp dichotomies such as good versus evil to define the nature of the cosmos, earthly life, and spiritual struggle.

Chosen People

The concept of "chosen people" is and always has been dangerous. Isaiah promised an imperial future in which Israel would enslave all other nations and all the wealth of the world would flow to Israel. God's promise to Abraham was less blatantly imperial. Abraham was to be the father of a great nation, which would be a blessing to all the nations. It didn't take long, however, for the story line to shift from universal to tribal blessing.

God ordered the extermination of all the people living in the land that the "chosen people" were meant to occupy according to divine fiat and with the aid of divine and human violence. If assessed in the context of real history, then this story is fanciful. If assessed in terms of its enduring theological legacy, then this story has profound and disturbing political consequences. Reform Jewish writer Regina Schwartz states:

> And what about the biblical narrative? Should we hold it culpable for emblazoning this desire for land acquisition on its readers, inscribing deep into our culture the primordial myth of an exodus that justifies conquest? From one perspective—that of history of the text—the conquest narrative is only a wild fantasy written by a powerless dispossessed people who dream of wondrous victories over their enemies, of living in a land where milk and honey flow, and of entering that land with the blessing and support of an Almighty Deity. But from another perspective—that of the text's political afterlife—there is another story that is less appealing and considerably less innocent, telling of creating a people through the massive displacement and destruction of other peoples, of laying claim to a land that had belonged to others, and of conducting this bloody conquest under the banner of divine will.[24]

A conquest narrative's "political afterlife" is most visible and damaging when it is linked to people with real power rather than fantasy power, when the desire for empire is matched by the capacity for and means to empire. This is certainly true for U.S. Empire, in which the conquest narrative shapes past and present policies and practices, including the extermination of Native Americans, Christian support for Zionism rooted in bizarre apocalyptic end-time scenarios involving the state of Israel, and the recent invasion of Iraq.[25]

A powerful empire that understands itself as chosen by God is by definition exceptional, and it often claims the right to use exceptional violence. Settlers who saw "their" land as the new Israel and themselves as God's new "chosen people" had little difficulty identifying native peoples with Canaanites, who could be exterminated like their biblical counterparts. Native American theologian and activist Robert Allen Warrior writes:

> Many Puritan preachers were fond of referring to Native Americans as Amalekites and Canaanites—in other words, people who, if they

would not be converted, were worthy of annihilation. By examining such instances in theological and political writings, in sermons, and elsewhere, we can understand how America's self-image as a "chosen people" has provided a rhetoric to mystify domination.[26]

Exceptionalist myths are at the heart of the U.S. "Crusader State" and, according to Kevin Phillips, evidence a "seething desire to take preemptive actions against" evil tyrants in the Middle East and elsewhere.[27] The United States, President Bush said, has a "special calling." "America is a nation with a mission, and that mission comes from our most basic beliefs." "This great republic will lead the cause of freedom." "The liberty we prize is not America's gift to the world. It is God's gift to the world." There "is wonder-working power, in the goodness and idealism and faith of the American people." We must "remember our calling as a blessed country is to make the world better." "This ideal of America is the hope of all mankind." In the official foreign-policy statement of the United States (NSS, National Security Strategy), as Claes G. Ryn wrote, President Bush "cited the exceptional and superior character of the United States as justifying its missionary role in the world."[28] "The desire for empire," Ryn observed, "is thus accompanied by a noble-sounding ideology for how to make the world better."[29]

Powerful Privileges

One of the deepest temptations within religious systems is to resort to a simplified view of the world, a view based on blessings and curses. This danger emerges in part out of biblical and theological portraits of God as all-powerful. God controls history; so when things go well, this implies divine favor, and when things go poorly, this reflects divine displeasure. Such a view is pervasive within the Bible even though it is contradicted numerous times by various prophets, the book of Job, and by Jesus. Powerful people seeking biblical justification for empire are not interested in and need not pay attention to these contradictions. All they need for their purposes is to cite any number of references from Abraham, Moses, Isaiah, and many other biblical personalities and stories that affirm that the fruits of fidelity according to God's promises are prosperity, greatness, defeat of enemies—in short, empire.

Being the world's most powerful empire can lead to a militarized commitment to maintain privileges that are understood not as the fruits of exploitation but rather signs of divine favor. "We are the number one nation," President Lyndon Johnson told the National Foreign Policy Conference at a crucial time during the Vietnam War, "and we are going to stay the number one nation."[30] In a speech to a convention of Junior Chamber of Commerce Executives in 1967, Johnson boasted:

> We own almost a third of the world's railroad tracks. We own almost two-thirds of the world's automobiles—and we don't have to wait three years to get a new one, either. . . . We own half the trucks in the world. We own almost a half of all the radios in the world. We own a third of all the electricity that is produced in the world. We own a fourth of all the steel. . . . Although we have only about 6% of the population of the world, we have half its wealth. Bear in mind that the other 94% of the population would like to trade with us. Maybe a better way of saying it would be that they would like to exchange places with us. I would like to see them enjoy the blessings that we enjoy. But don't you help them exchange places with us—because I don't want to be where they are. Instead, I believe that we are generous enough—I believe that we are compassionate enough—I believe that we are grateful enough that we would like to see all of them enjoy the blessings that are ours.[31]

Christians living in the U.S. Empire can be easily seduced. We are tempted to see the maldistribution of the earth's goods as divine blessing rather than the tainted fruits of unjust systems. We are also prone to supporting foreign policies to defend the present distribution of goods. Christian support for destructive empire, therefore, runs far deeper than its firm base among legalistic Christians. "The dominant values of American life—affluence, achievement, appearance, power, competition, consumption, individualism—are vastly different from anything recognizably Christian," the Jesus scholar Marcus Borg wrote. "As individuals and as a culture our existence has become massively idolatrous."

Violent Power

Biblical perspectives on power also have been adapted and applied in ways that serve U.S. Empire. Unfortunately, the most enduring and damaging legacy of the Bible, the Quran, and the monotheistic faith traditions they inspire may be violence. Power, according to these "sacred" texts, is violent and coercive. The way God proves to be God is through superior violence. The three main biblical story lines position earthly and/or heavenly hope in God's violence. Violence—whether liberating, punishing, or vindicating—is the key to justice within or at the end of history. Many Christians claim to have broken with these views by revering a crucified Lord, but their interpretations of Jesus' life and death through apocalyptic lenses betray that claim. The crucified Lord is expected to return as apocalyptic judge.

The belief that superior violence saves is today so prominent that violence has in fact become the dominant world religion. Walter Wink says that violence "is the ethos of our times" and the "spirituality of the modern world." Violence is "accorded the status of a religion, demanding from its devotees an absolute obedience to death." Wink says the "roots of this devotion to violence are deep," and that violence, "not Christianity, is the real religion of America."[32] The United States would not have become the most militarized country in the history of the world, would not spend more money on the military than the rest of the world combined, would not have many hundreds of military bases encircling the globe, and would not have its soldiers on the ground in more than 150 countries—all this would not have happened unless violence had functionally replaced God within the religious system of most U.S. Christians.

Although these statements concerning God and violence are painful to write and to contemplate, they still understate the problem. Violence today is God, the one and only functional God at the heart of most theologies and most ideologies, whether capitalist, Marxist, anarchist, revolutionary, reactionary, or religious. In the secular world, superior violence is God because violence is presumed to be the only and ultimate means to security, victory, or revenge. In the religious world, violence has overtaken God in terms of loyalty and ultimate allegiance. The Bible, the Quran, and monotheistic faith say that superior violence saves. Proclaiming God Almighty and restricting God to One whose power is understood as superior violence mean that in monotheistic religion *violence is God because violence saves God* by establishing and maintaining God's credibility. In the world of empire, violence is the practical means by which one fulfills a divine mission. But because faith in the utility of violence is pervasive, it can be said that violence itself is God. One reason I choose to be a Christian is because Jesus, as we shall see in chapter 8, undermines links between God and violence.

Violent Power and the Recent History of Empire

Violent power has particularly devastating consequences when linked to the goals, strategies, and presumptions of U.S. Empire. Linking imperial power to chosenness, presumed goodness, and to the biblical worldview that pits good against evil is a prescription for spiraling violence and permanent holy war.

The recent history of U.S. Empire has fueled a spiral of violence. Following World War II the United States secured economic privileges at the expense of others. Throughout much of the Third World, it maintained stability without development while denigrating people, democracy, and human rights. It militarized its foreign policy and put compliant governments in place, secured control of oil, and established rules for the global economy that benefited itself while impoverishing others. It met inevitable backlashes with violence. Military advantages afforded by the absence of a rival superpower fueled fantasies and spawned strategies for permanent supremacy.

Biblical themes guided and aided these pursuits and defenses of empire. Many U.S. leaders and citizens of empire, including Christians, convinced themselves, if not others, that they were a chosen people and a nation with a divine mission. They embraced biblical notions that power is rooted in superior violence and that salvation is manifested in defeat of enemies. They accepted the worldview that said history, the United States, and the cosmos were engulfed in a deadly conflict in which the forces of good and evil vied for supremacy. This justified implementation of a grand strategy aimed at turning present advantages into permanent empire based on militarization of space and unending military superiority. The U.S. power itself was understood, as parts of the Bible suggested, as a visible sign of God's blessing. The prominence of the United States in world affairs vindicated Christian faith in the midst of empire and vice versa. Chosen by God, the United States and its people could not refuse their noble mission without betraying a sacred trust. U.S. military superiority and its application in the struggle against the forces of darkness were part and parcel of a divine mission. Salvation involved defeat of communism, terrorism, and evil itself. It depended on us. "We've come to know truths that we will never question," President Bush reminded us. "Evil is real, and it must be opposed." We know that "history has matched this nation with this time," and "that our responsibility to history is already clear: to answer these attacks and rid the world of evil." We know also "that God is not neutral between them."

Christianity's embrace of U.S. Empire is rooted in numerous biblical themes that have been adopted and adapted to serve imperial goals. Violent images of God and violent explanations for history dominate the Bible. They find their most damaging and visible expressions in the contemporary theologies and practices of the so-called Christian Right. Legalistic Christianity serves militarized empire; it undermines the credibility of Christianity itself, and its theocratic tendencies threaten the republic as well.

The problem of Christianity and violent empire, however, has deeper roots. For a long time U.S. Empire has seduced Christians with material benefits, impressive rhetoric, and alluring violence. Meanwhile, violent images of God not only feed the extremist fantasies of religious fanatics; they also are featured centrally in traditional Christian theologies, worship, music, and liturgies that must be challenged.[33] Violence is the rule, not the exception, whether we are speaking of U.S. Empire, the Bible, fundamentalist, or mainstream Christianity.

The tragic legacy of violent God and violent religion rooted in "sacred text" is not only that religion inevitably, if unconsciously, is reduced to violence. It is also our inability to see or embrace the reality and potential of nonviolent power. There is a nonviolent, anti-imperial "mustard-seed" Christian tradition linked to the historical Jesus.[34] It roots nonviolence in Jesus' nonviolence and in his testimony to the nonviolent power of God. The "mustard seed" stream of Christianity views nonviolent power as an effective means to resist evil and to overcome injustice. This stream, if taken seriously, can help the nation transition from empire to republic, and it can help transform imperial Christianity into a vital force for transformation.

Notes

1. Claes G. Ryn, *America the Virtuous* (New Brunswick, NJ: Transaction, 2003), 352.

2. Chalmers Johnson, *The Sorrows of Empire: Militarism, Secrecy, and the End of the Republic* (New York: Metropolitan Books, 2004), 287.

3. Marcus J. Borg, *Jesus: A New Vision* (San Francisco: Harper & Row, 1987), 195.

4. Bruce Bawer, *Stealing Jesus: How Fundamentalism Betrays Christianity* (New York: Crown, 1997), 10, with emphasis in original.

5. Quoted in Laurie Goodstein, "After the Attacks: Finding Fault; Falwell's Finger-Pointing Inappropriate, Bush Says," *New York Times,* September 15, 2001.

6. Quoted in Bruce Lincoln, *Holy Terrors: Thinking about Religion after September 11* (Chicago: Chicago University Press, 2003), 46.

7. Kevin Phillips, *American Dynasty: Aristocracy, Fortune, and the Politics of Deceit in the House of Bush* (New York: Vintage, 2004), 5.

8. Ibid., 317, 221, 242.

9. Bawer, *Stealing Jesus,* 100.

10. Ibid., 100–2.

11. David D. Kirkpatrick, "Wrath and Mercy: The Return of the Warrior Jesus," *New York Times,* April 4, 2004, Sunday, Late Edition—Final.

12. Phillips, *American Dynasty,* 233.

13. Lincoln, *Holy Terrors,* 31–32.

14. Quoted in Bawer, *Stealing Jesus,* 8–9, with emphasis in original.

15. Joe Bageant, "The Covert Kingdom: Thy Will Be Done, on Earth as It Is in Texas," *Dissent Voice,* May 18, 2004, www.dissidentvoice.org/May04.htm.

16. Quoted in Phillips, *American Dynasty,* 212.

17. Ibid., 235.

18. See Jack Nelson-Pallmeyer, *Jesus against Christianity: Reclaiming the Missing Jesus* (Harrisburg, PA: Trinity Press International, 2001), chs. 13–16. See also John Dominic Crossan, *Jesus: A Revolutionary Biography* (New York: HarperCollins, 1994).

19. Crossan, *Jesus: A Revolutionary Biography,* 1–2.

20. See Richard Horsley, ed., *Paul and Empire: Religion and Power in Roman Imperial Society* (Harrisburg, PA: Trinity Press International, 1997). See also John Dominic Crossan and Jonathan L. Reed, *In Search of Paul: The New Quest to Understand His World and Words* (New York: HarperCollins, 2004).

21. John Driver, *How Christians Made Peace with War* (Scottdale, PA: Herald Press, 1988), 14–15.

22. Ibid., 30, 32.

23. Ibid., 13.

24. Regina M. Schwartz, *The Curse of Cain: The Violent Legacy of Monotheism* (Chicago: University of Chicago Press, 1997), 57.

25. Fundamentalist Christians are among Israel's most prominent supporters, including support for Israeli policies that deny rights and land to the Palestinians. This support is theologically grounded. They believe God gave this land to the people of Israel, and that a state of Israel firmly established is a prerequisite for the second coming of Christ and for Armageddon.

26. Robert Allen Warrior, "A Native American Perspective: Canaanites, Cowboys, and Indians," in *Voices from the Margin: Interpreting the Bible in the Third World* (ed. R. S. Sugirtharajah; Maryknoll, NY: Orbis Books, 1991), 293.

27. Phillips, *American Dynasty,* 60–61, borrows this term from Professor Walter McDougall.

28. Ryn, *America the Virtuous,* 7.

29. Ibid., 4.

30. Quoted in Richard J. Barnet, *The Roots of War* (Baltimore: Penguin Books, 1971), 152.

31. *Baltimore Sun,* June 28, 1967.

32. Walter Wink, *Engaging the Powers: Discernment and Resistance in a World of Domination* (Minneapolis: Fortress, 1992), 13.

33. Bret Hesla and I have recently published a book modeling theology, liturgy, and music that purges Christianity of violent images of God and builds on the example of Jesus' nonviolence. See Jack Nelson-Pallmeyer and Bret Hesla, *Worship in the Spirit of Jesus: Theology, Liturgy, and Songs without Violence* (Cleveland: Pilgrim, 2005).

34. Some examples of historical Jesus scholarship include: Marcus Borg, *Jesus: A New Vision* (San Francisco: Harper & Row, 1987); Crossan, *Jesus: A Revolutionary Biography*; Robert W. Funk et al., *The Five Gospels: What Did Jesus Really Say?* (Santa Rosa: Polebridge, 1993); and Nelson-Pallmeyer, *Jesus against Christianity.*

ALTERNATIVES TO VIOLENCE

"You have heard that it was said, 'You shall love your neighbor and hate your enemy.' But I say to you, Love your enemies and pray for those who persecute you, so that you may be children of your Father in heaven, . . . [who] makes his sun rise on the evil and on the good, and sends rain on the righteous and on the unrighteous."

—Jesus (in Matt 5:43–45)

People, groups, and governments will not renounce violence when that is seen to mean becoming powerless and helpless in a conflict in which their basic beliefs and the nature of their society are, or are believed to be, under attack. In acute conflicts in order for war and other violence not to be used as the final means of action to advance or defend one's principles, ideals, society, or existence, some other means of strong action need be available. There has to be a substitute means of conducting the conflict powerfully with the chance of success equivalent to or greater than the violent option.

—Gene Sharp[1]

A Smorgasbord of Options

The Bible isn't a monolithic book. It offers competing and irreconcilable portraits and stories about God, faith, and history. People of faith choose from a smorgasbord of options, including from both pro and anti-imperial streams within the Bible. Nearly all of the Bible's story lines, however, privilege violent understandings of power and root hope in the liberating, punishing, or vindicating violence of God. We are so accustomed to equating power and salvation with violence that it is nearly impossible for us to consider alternatives.

The historical Jesus' radical nonviolence challenges many of the core assumptions of the biblical writers and perhaps our own.[2] This includes his rejection of violent images of God and violent explanations of history that guided them as well as assumptions about violent power. The passages I describe below are embedded in a book that overwhelmingly rejects the individual and collective weight of the arguments of these passages in favor of violence-of-God traditions and violent expectations of history. The nonviolent, anti-imperial stream connected to Jesus, in other words, is *a minority voice.* It is contradicted and/or marginalized within the Hebrew Scriptures, the Gospels, the New Testament, and in the Christian tradition as a whole. Each privileges violence-of-God traditions and violent expectations of history.

A nonviolent, anti-imperial stream associated with the historical Jesus *is* evident within the Gospels, however, and Christians arguably should take it seriously. Jesus' radical and practical nonviolence—when coupled with subsequent nonviolent theory and tactics faithful to it—offer alternative ways to confront injustice, including what seem to be an empire's overwhelming economic, military, and ideological advantages and power. Christians must choose between imperial and anti-imperial Christianity, between violent or nonviolent Christianity, and between a Christianity rooted in grandiose or modest "mustard-seed" expectations. A nonviolent anti-imperial stream associated with the historical Jesus can help inform our choices about empire and republic as well as about Christianity itself.

Imperial Boasting

Empires presume divine favor. The U.S. leaders, for example, state or imply that the United States is blessed by God because it is a "Christian" nation. The country's wealth and power are understood as material blessings that confirm the rightness of both the Bible and Christian practice. These blessings, including empire itself, are understood to be threatened by deviance, which helps explain theocratic tendencies within the religious body politic.

The tendency to view empire as the fruit of fidelity is not limited to the United States. It was visible during the zenith of other empires. Karen

Armstrong writes approvingly of God and empire in reference to the Quran and Islam in the seventh century:

> Under Umar's leadership . . . the Arabs burst into Iraq, Syria and Egypt, achieving a series of astonishing victories. They overcame the Persian army at the Battle of Qadisiyyah (637), which led to the fall of the capital of the Persian Sassanids at Ctesiphon. As soon as they had the manpower, Muslims would thus be able to occupy the whole of the Persian Empire. They encountered stiffer resistance in the Byzantine Empire, and conquered no territory in the Byzantine heartlands in Anatolia. Nevertheless, the Muslims were victorious at the Battle of Yarmuk (636) in northern Palestine, conquered Jerusalem in 638, and controlled the whole of Syria, Palestine and Egypt by 641. The Muslim armies went on to seize the North African coast as far as Cyrenaica. Just twenty years after the Battle of Badr [Muslims inflicted a dramatic military defeat on the Meccans at the Battle of Badr in 624], the Arabs found themselves in possession of a sizeable empire. This expansion continued. A century after the Prophet's death, the Islamic Empire extended from the Pyrenees to the Himalayas. It seemed yet another miracle and sign of God's favour. Before the coming of Islam, the Arabs had been a despised outgroup; but in a remarkably short space of time they had inflicted major defeats upon two world empires. The experience of conquest enhanced their sense that something tremendous had happened to them. . . . Their success also endorsed the message of the Quran, which had asserted that a correctly guided society must prosper because it was in tune with God's laws. Look what had happened once they had surrendered to God's will![3]

The presumption that empire proved God's favor was also evident in the writings of the aristocratic Jewish historian Josephus, a Jewish leader who was captured by Rome during the First Roman-Jewish War of 66 to 73 CE. During captivity, he tried to convince his fellow Jews that to resist Rome was to resist God:

> Fortune, indeed, had from all quarters passed over to them [the Romans], and God who went the round of the nations, bringing to each in turn the rod of empire, now rested over Italy. . . . You are warring not against the Romans only, but also against God. . . . The

Deity has fled from the holy places and taken His stand on the side of those with whom you are now at war.[4]

A fine line separates the view that superior violence is God from the idea that says superior violence is proof that God has bestowed "the rod of empire." Whether one sees in empire or in empire's boastings, gain or loss, truth or hypocrisy, God or human haughtiness, depends on one's experience. Virgil, a poet of Roman imperial arrogance, wrote in the *Aeneid*:

> *Roman, remember by your strength to rule*
> *Earth's peoples—for your arts are to be these:*
> *To pacify, to impose the rule of law,*
> *To spare the conquered, battle down the proud.*

A rebel general Calgacus offered a far different description of the Roman Empire in the first century:

> Robbers of the world, now that earth fails their all-devastating hands, they probe even the sea; if their enemy have wealth, they have greed; if he be poor, they are ambitious; East nor West has glutted them; alone of mankind they covet with the same passion want [poor lands] as much as wealth [rich lands]. To plunder, butcher, steal, these things they misname empire: they make a desolation and they call it peace.[5]

Closer to home the *Voice of America* broadcasting was known within the United States as a voice for freedom, but in some settings it was understood as a mouthpiece for U.S. propaganda. Brazilian bishop and poet Pedro Casadaliga's wrote in the context of destructive U.S. Empire in Latin America in the 1980s:

> *People should realize*
> *That this is the Voice of those who have a voice*
> *Because they have their dollars*
> *And they have the power to kill, with a button,*
> *the whole human race*
> *and under their own roof the power*
> *to kill, day by day, with counterinformation*
> *their own sickly conscience.*[6]

Peel away imperial rhetoric and you are likely to find destructive empire. John Dominic Crossan asks: "How do oppressed people react to overbearing cultural seductiveness, overpowering military superiority, overwhelming economic exploitation, and overweening social discrimination? One way," he writes, "is simply to fight and lose, fight and lose, again and again and again."[7]

The Spiral of Violence at the Heart of the Bible

Biblical violence is cyclical and seemingly without end. God creates the earth, including humans, but after "the earth is filled with violence because of them," God violently destroys the earth and most of its inhabitants (Gen 6:13; 7:23). Joseph uses food as a weapon on behalf of the Egyptian Empire. All Egyptians end up penniless, landless, and enslaved (Gen 47). Resentments flower. A new Pharaoh takes control and retaliates. Hatreds explode, and violence thrives and survives numerous reversals. No longer privileged, the Israelites, according to the biblical script, groan amid their oppression. They cry out and, with God's help, win (Exodus). In the aftermath of Pharaoh's defeat, the Israelites steal land and commit "divinely sanctioned" genocide.

The people settle in the land they have stolen, behave badly, and displease God, who helps foreign nations to conquer them. Israelites sent into exile are unable to sing the Lord's song in captivity and expectantly wait for the happy day when they will smash the heads of their captor's children against the rocks (Ps 137:4, 9). Isaiah announces that exile isn't permanent. God one day will come "with vengeance," "save" the people, and "spare no one" (35:4; 47:3). With God's help the oppressed will become oppressors. Daniel refuses an imperial decree and is thrown into a lions' den. He is protected by God, walks away, and immediately "those who had accused Daniel were brought and thrown into the den of lions—they, their children, and their wives. Before they reached the bottom of the den the lions overpowered them and broke all their bones in pieces" (Dan 6:24).

In the New Testament Mary anticipates the day when God will bring down the powerful from their thrones, lift up the lowly, fill the hungry with good things, and send the rich away empty (Luke 1:52–53). Powerful Jews, however, collaborate with Roman oppressors. Both stay in power by crucifying subversives like Jesus. Meanwhile, the centuries-long effort to get right with God continues. Jews make many attempts to please God in the hope that doing so will stop God's punishment and trigger God's liberating violence. Nothing works until, in a bizarre plot twist, Jesus is crucified and rises from the dead. His blood sacrifice is said to please and appease God, but Roman imperialism flourishes nonetheless. The New Testament writers tell believers not to fret, however, because Jesus will return soon as an apocalyptic end-time judge. Rome will be destroyed, the world will end as we know it, the faithful will be vindicated, and evildoers punished. Ironically, the Jesus who taught love of enemies will oversee the destruction of most of humanity.

Jesus and the Spiral of Violence

Rome's oppressive power affected all aspects of life in first-century Palestine. Its system of taxes, tribute, and commercialization of land impoverished many peasants. Its brutality featured massacres and crucifixions of potential and actual rebels. Its propaganda included promotion of the emperor cult and Rome's "Gospel" of peace through military conquest. Imperial rule depended on Rome-appointed client-kings and co-opted temple elites backed by Roman military power. Legions of Roman soldiers were ready, if called upon, to crush any and all opposition when client kings or temple elites failed in carrying out their appointed duties. The "Roman response to such a situation was massive military action and the crucifixion of all common people who had taken part, and a rendering of accounts from the respective aristocracies."[8]

Jews and Christians rejected the idea that empire reflected God's will and blessing, as the strength of the anti-imperial stream within the Bible testifies. Their strategies for challenging empire, however, were dangerous and ineffective. They distorted hope by projecting God's violence as the solution to the problem of empire. Hope in first-century Palestine, for example, was predicated on God sending a military Messiah who would assist the people's violent struggle, defeat the empire's armies, free Israel, and perhaps fulfill Isaiah's vision of Israel becoming God's powerful, wealthy, dominant nation. This approach to countering empire led people to "fight and lose, fight and lose, again and again and again."

The other "strategy" for challenging empire evident in first-century Palestine and beyond was to wait and prepare for the apocalyptic violence of God that would soon end history and vindicate the faithful. John the Baptist is depicted in the Gospels as an apocalyptic prophet announcing the imminent end of the world. John was executed under orders from a Roman client king, but his fantasies refused to die with him. The Gospel writers and much of subsequent Christianity assigned meaning to Jesus' life and death in reference to violent images of God that Jesus himself rejected. They portrayed Jesus' death as an atoning sacrifice that appeased a punishing deity and/or as part of God's plan for history's inevitable plunge into a bloody apocalypse, including Armageddon and final judgment. The nonviolent Jesus would return as violent judge.

The theologies of the Gospel writers made little sense to most Jews but caught on among Gentiles. They said in a nutshell that Jesus was the long-awaited Messiah sent by God to save Israel and all believers. The people who had expected a military Messiah to defeat empire within history, however, had been wrong. Jesus' blood sacrifice effectively appeased God, but Jesus' death and resurrection were part of God's imminent apocalyptic plan. Oppressive empires would be destroyed, the world would end, and the faithful would be vindicated within the lifetime of most believers, as Christ returned to oversee a final judgment.

When telling their various Jesus stories, the Gospel writers included historical material about Jesus that strongly suggests that he said no to empire itself and to the violent "solutions" to the problem of empire. Jesus rejected the violent images of God and expectations of history that dominate the Bible, including expectations of messianic or apocalyptic violence, and the need to appease God with an atoning sacrifice. This historical material reflects a nonviolent mustard-seed view of Jesus, which is the basis of an alternative Christianity countering both destructive empire and the illusionary fantasies that empires will be defeated with divine or human violence within or at the end of history.

Mustard Seeds and Other Surprising Passages

In *Jesus against Christianity*, I wrote in detail about Jesus' clash with Christianity.[9] In *Worship in the Spirit of Jesus*, Bret Hesla and I have also offered examples of what a re-ritualized Christianity might look like when faithful to the nonviolence of Jesus.[10] Here let me describe insights from ten passages that make up the core of Jesus' nonviolent approach to resisting empire.

First, Jesus teaches love of enemies (Matt 5:43–45). This is among the most radical and most unexpected teachings in the Bible. Hatred of enemies is implied on page after page, and the overwhelming definition of salvation is defeat of enemies within or at the end of history. John Dominic Crossan comments on Jesus' radical call to love enemies: "I can only interpret it as commanding absolute nonviolence."[11]

Second, Jesus lampoons salvation as defeat of enemies by telling a story in which a hated enemy saves a beaten Jew (Luke 10:29–37). According to the parable of the "compassionate Samaritan," we are saved by our enemies. Walter Wink explains that the gift our enemies bring to us is that they *see aspects of ourselves that we cannot discover any other way than through our enemies."* [12]

Third, Jesus exposes the spiral of violence in a parable about peasant revolt (Mark 12:1–9). A wealthy absentee owner sends workers and his son to collect his crop only to have the peasants beat or kill them. The owner is poised to retaliate with brutal violence. Peasants had good reason to resent wealthy landowners. They were hired to work their former lands as tenants raising a new owner's export crop. As the parable unfolds, one senses the exhilaration of oppressed tenants living vicariously through its telling. The humiliated humiliate others. The shamed do the shaming. The ones considered disposable kill and dispose of the body of the owner's son. The disinherited rightful heirs to the land deny the inheritance of an illegitimate heir. There must have been a feeling of power as oppression gave way to rebellion and the vicarious experience of justified revenge.

Had the parable ended there, Jesus' hearers may have joined together and gone on a rampage against any deserving oppressor. But Jesus' parable includes an ominous question and response: "What then will the owner of the vineyard do? He will come and destroy the tenants and give the vineyard to others." The parable highlights the spiral of violence, underscores the futility of violent rebellion, and leaves one groping for alternative forms of protest and resistance. [13]

Fourth, Jesus teaches a model for creative nonviolent action. In Matthew 5:38–42 Jesus says:

> "You have heard that it was said, 'An eye for an eye and a tooth for a tooth.' But I say to you, Do not [use violence when you] resist an evildoer. But if anyone strikes you on the right cheek, turn the other also; and if anyone wants to sue you and take your coat, give your cloak as well; and if anyone forces you to go one mile, go also the second mile. Give to everyone who begs from you, and do not refuse anyone who wants to borrow from you."

Jesus offers exploited people in first-century Palestine three examples of creative nonviolent resistance to oppression. Slapping, suing, and forcing involve someone with power taking advantage of vulnerable people. The question in each case, Wink stresses, "is how the oppressed can recover the initiative and assert their human dignity in a situation that cannot for the time being be changed."[14] Wink explains the situation and reasons for Jesus' counsel:

> A backhand slap was the usual way of admonishing inferiors. Masters backhanded slaves; husbands, wives; parents, children; Romans, Jews. *We have here a set of unequal relations, in each of which retaliation would invite retribution.* The only normal response would be cowering submission. . . . There are among his hearers people who were subjected to these very indignities, forced to stifle outrage at their dehumanizing treatment by the hierarchical system of class, race, gender, age, and status, and as a result of imperial occupation. Why then does he counsel these already humiliated people to turn the other cheek? Because this action robs the oppressor of the power to humiliate. . . . The person who turns the other cheek is saying, in effect, "Try again. Your first blow failed to achieve its intended effect. I deny you the power to humiliate me. I am a human being just like you. Your status does not alter that fact. You cannot demean me."[15]

This unexpected behavior in a world of honor and shame, Wink comments, "would create enormous difficulties for the striker." He could escalate the conflict by turning it into a fistfight, but this would make "the other his equal. . . . He has been given notice that this underling is in fact a human being."[16]

The other nonviolent actions encouraged by Jesus reflect similar dynamics. If the powerful sue you and take your outer garment, then give them your underwear. Stand naked before the court, shame the system, and humiliate all who look upon you. If a Roman soldier forces you to carry his pack the legally prescribed one mile, then keep going and get *him* into trouble. These may not constitute dramatic victories, but—like Rosa Parks refusing to give up her bus seat—they are something. As Wink states, It "is in the context of Roman military occupation that Jesus speaks" and with full awareness "of the futility of armed insurrection against Roman imperial might."[17]

Fifth, Jesus compares the reign of God to a mustard seed (Mark 4:30–32). Mustard seed as metaphor flies in the face of theological, historical, and mythological expectations of salvation or historical vindication through God's violence. It clashes sharply with Isaiah's imperial promises and with conventional wisdom that said the arrival of God's realm would be dramatic, even cataclysmic. "For Jesus, God's domain was a modest affair, not a new world empire," comments the Jesus Seminar. "It was pervasive but unrecognized, rather than noisy and arresting."[18] We often miss another radical aspect of the mustard-seed metaphor as described by Crossan:

> The mustard plant is dangerous even when domesticated in the garden, and is deadly when growing wild in the grain fields. . . . The point, in other words, is not just that the mustard plant starts as a proverbially small seed and grows into a shrub. . . . It is that it tends to take over where it is not wanted. . . . And that, said Jesus, was what the Kingdom was like. Like a pungent shrub with dangerous take-over properties.[19]

Jesus suggests that people of faith are to be communities of subversive weeds that subvert the goals of those who plant imperial gardens.

Sixth, Jesus looks at the unjust world of first-century Palestine and sees abundance rather than scarcity, and the abundance he sees is rooted in the abundance of God (Matt 6:25–30). Jesus walks hand-in-hand with the marginalized, and he challenges the imperial system that is responsible for their poverty. As he does so, he sees the possibility of abundant life rooted in the abundance of God. It is the reality of God's abundance that makes injustice so offensive. Injustice betrays God's character and God's intentions for humanity and creation. The reality of God is abundant love. Jesus experiences God infinitely giving. He tells a parable of a great dinner to which all are invited "and there is still room" (Luke 14:15–24). This abundance is in stark contrast to the scarcity of goods and blessing presumed by legalistic and many traditional Christians. Against the covenant's limited blessing in which rain is a conditional blessing linked to obedience (Lev 26:3–4), Jesus says that God makes the sun rise on the evil and the good, and sends rain on the righteous and the unrighteous (Matt 5:45). This is simply the way God is. God's abundance is at the heart of our invitation to love enemies, to share goods, and to engage in creative active nonviolence to resist empire, counter oppression, or seek justice (Matt 5:38–45).

God's abundance and our embrace of abundant life should not be equated with riches or affluence (Mark 10:17–25) but with mindfulness and sufficiency. The God who provides for the birds and gives us the miraculous beauty of the lilies wants us to notice. God provides abundance sufficient for all. "That's why I tell you: Don't fret about your life—

what you're going to eat and drink—or about your body—what you're going to wear. There is more to living than food and clothing, isn't there?" (Matt 6:31, paraphrased). The Buddhist peacemaker Thich Nhat Hanh describes mindfulness and captures the essence of Jesus' vision in these words: "When we are mindful touching deeply the present moment, we can see and listen deeply and the fruits are always understanding, acceptance, love, and the desire to relieve suffering and bring joy."[20]

Seventh, Jesus' parable of the Prodigal Son models God's unlimited grace and represents a dramatic reversal of expectations concerning the punishing character of God (Luke 15:11–32). A father's younger son departs and squanders his inheritance. He returns, but before he can ask for mercy, the father puts celebratory plans in motion. The boy's father "was filled with compassion; he ran and put his arms around him and kissed him" (v. 20). In this parable Jesus shatters expectations of a punishing Deity. He portrays God as the source of unlimited and undeserved compassion. Forgiveness is, according to Jesus, the character of God. Forgiveness is available to us without our asking. Jesus experiences God as infinitely giving and forgiving and invites us to imitate the unlimited forgiveness of God (Matt 18:22).

Eighth, Jesus further jettisons notions of a punishing God in a parable about a banquet in which judgment is understood as self-exclusion and not the action of a violent, punishing deity (Luke 14:16–24). According to the prophets, God orchestrates the destruction of Israel and reduces the people to cannibalism as punishment for sin. Matthew's Jesus threatens people with eternal fires and weeping and gnashing of teeth. The book of Revelation describes those who will "drink the wine of God's wrath, poured unmixed into the cup of his anger" so as to be "tormented with fire and sulfur in the presence of the holy angels and in the presence of the Lamb" (14:10). In sharp contrast, this parable moves markedly in the direction of envisioning God's noncoercive power. Instead of threats and a scarcity of God's blessing, we have an open invitation to dinner that includes everybody. Not everyone accepts the invitation, but exclusion from dinner is the choice of those who are preoccupied with other things. According to this parable, judgment is by self-exclusion. If we miss the beckoning of the Spirit and make bad choices, then we miss abundant life. I call this "invitational judgment" because abundant life and whether others have a decent life depends on acceptance or rejection of an invitation that is open to all and always available. Invitational judgment suggests that God's power can't force us or others to live justly or punish us or others for being unjust. Acceptance or refusal of the invitation to abundant life has consequences for us and others, but God's invitational power excludes the punishing sanctions of a violent deity.

Ninth, Jesus rejects the idea that a Messiah will come to save the people. Jews expected, and occasionally announced the arrival of, a Messiah in Israel to reestablish Israel's privileged and powerful place among the nations, purge the defiled land of imperialism, and replace the temple's priestly rulers, collaborating with the foreign oppressors. Jesus dismisses these anti-imperial expectations rooted in violence. The Temptation narrative (Matt 4:1–11; Luke 4:1–13) indicates that Jesus rejects messianic expectations and their implicit and explicit understandings of God and history. No wonder-worker sent by God would miraculously end hunger, inspire proper belief, or rule over Israel and the nations.

Jesus' rejection of the popular idea that a Messiah will free Israel is also a likely interpretation of the parable of an unmerciful servant who has his debts forgiven but refuses to reciprocate (Matt 18:23–35). The Jewish Messiah was expected to cancel debts as part of the overthrow of the oppressive system. "The opening scene of the parable," William Herzog writes, "depicts a messianic moment. . . . If the largest amount of debt imaginable has been canceled, then the messianic king has arrived and the messianic age has begun."[21] The messianic moment unravels quickly because oppression is rooted in an entrenched, exploitative bureaucracy. Jesus understands that although oppressed people long for, need, and deserve justice, hope rooted in a Messiah is false hope that stifles authentic hope. It is a great and tragic irony that, with the aid of Gospel distortions, Christianity has turned Jesus into a largely otherworldly Messiah after Jesus' own life, faith, and experience of God led him to reject messianic expectations.

Finally, Jesus stresses the present nature of God's presence and rejects apocalyptic expectations. Asked by the Pharisees when the "kingdom of God" is coming, Jesus answers, "The kingdom of God is not coming with things that can be observed; nor will they say, 'Look, here it is!' or 'There it is!' For, in fact, the kingdom of God is among you" (Luke 17:20–21). Jesus doesn't root hope in promises that a violent God will replace or destroy oppressive systems in the near or distant future. He plants his life, his hope, and his nonviolence in the nonviolent character of God already present. God's Spirit, Jesus suggests, surrounds us every minute of every day and invites us here, now, everywhere, and always to nonviolently resist injustice and to embrace abundant life in the alternative realm of God.

Thus, the images of God and the actions and words of Jesus described above include love of enemies, salvation through enemies, breaking the spiral of violence, creative nonviolent action, the call to be subversive weeds, abundance, unlimited grace, invitational power, and a nonviolent God. *None of these images* can be reconciled with sacrificial or apocalyptic interpretations of Jesus that frame mainstream Christianity, much less the wrathful images of God that dominate the end-time fantasies of legalistic Christians. The nonviolence of Jesus offers Christians an alternative foundation from which to challenge U.S. Empire, to resist evil, and to work for justice. It also presents people with an alternative set of values and presuppositions concerning God's character and the nature of power, an understanding for grounding Christian faith and action.

Nonviolent Action

The nonviolent anti-imperial stream linked to the historical Jesus challenges common assumptions concerning the nature of divine and human power that dominate today's political, ideological, and religious landscapes. It offers the possibility that Christians—sickened by violence, disgusted by U.S. Empire, and yet concerned about injustice, terrorism, and war—might pay attention to the power of nonviolence. Just because nonviolence is rooted in an understanding of power that rejects killing and bloodshed doesn't mean it is not subversive, powerful, or dangerous to those who benefit from injustice. Nonviolence, Gene Sharp argues, is "a realistic alternative to war and other violence."[22] He acknowledges, however, that in order to convince others that nonviolence is a "functional alternative [it] must be able to deal satisfactorily with the 'hard cases' for which violence has in the past been believed to be required." These hard cases "include conflicts against dictatorships, foreign invasions and occupations, internal usurpations, oppression, attempted genocide, and mass expulsions and killings."[23] No easy task, Sharp says, but doable. History offers examples of successful nonviolence in relation to each of the "hard cases" above.

Sharp lays out the case for the effectiveness of nonviolent struggle based on the following assumptions:

First, nonviolence is powerful. Throughout history in "a great variety of situations, across centuries and cultural barriers," nonviolent forms of struggle have been applied and have shown "the ability to be stubborn and to resist powerful opponents powerfully." Determined, disciplined nonviolent action has succeeded against "ruthless opponents" that applied "extreme repression."

Second, power is rooted in the cooperation or noncooperation of people and institutions. Nonviolent struggle can succeed against tyrants and dictators because "the strength of even dictatorships is dependent on sources of power in the society, which in turn depend on the cooperation of a multitude of institutions and people—cooperation which may or may not continue." Sharp explains:

> Noncooperation and defiance subvert the needed obedience and cooperation that supply the necessary sources of power. For example, rejection of the ruler's legitimacy reduces a crucial reason for obedience by both aides and the general populace. Extensive popular disobedience and defiance creates immense enforcement problems. Massive strikes can paralyze the economy. Widespread administrative noncooperation of the bureaucracy can thwart governmental operations. Mutinies of the opponents' police and troops can dissolve the opponents' capacity to repress nonviolent resisters and to maintain their regime.[24]

Third, disciplined nonviolence can thwart the violence and repression of opponents. Coercive, violent power, including repression, is meant to silence and intimidate people into submission. Sharp describes a dynamic within nonviolent struggle by which repression weakens rather than strengthens those who use it:

> Severe repression may initiate a special process called "political jiu-jitsu." The opponents' difficulties in dealing with nonviolent action are primarily associated with the special dynamics and processes of this technique. It is designed to operate against opponents able and willing to use violent sanctions. However, political struggle by means of nonviolent action against violent repression creates a special, asymmetrical, conflict situation. The nonviolent resisters can use the asymmetry of nonviolent means versus violent action in order to apply to their opponents a political operation analogous to the Japanese martial art of jiu-jitsu. The contrast in types of action throws the opponents off balance politically, causing their repression to rebound against their position and weaken their power. By

remaining nonviolent while continuing the struggle, the resisters will improve their own position.[25]

Finally, nonviolent struggle involves a great variety of strategies and tactics that make it effective in diverse settings. Sharp identifies 198 methods of nonviolent action used successfully throughout history, including teach-ins, strikes, sit-ins, boycotts, marches, and guerrilla theater. He organizes these methods in relation to three categories: protest and persuasion, non-cooperation, and nonviolent intervention.[26] Successful nonviolent struggle requires strategic planning, casting off fear, discipline, persistence, effective leadership, clearly articulated goals, and an understanding of nonviolent theory, strategy, and tactics. Sharp describes four successful outcomes:

> In cases of success, the change may come as a result of one of four mechanisms. Rarely, as a result of nonviolent struggle, changes in attitude have led the opponents to make concessions voluntarily because it is right to do so—*conversion.* Far more often, the with-drawal of economic or political cooperation has forced the opponents to agree to compromise—*accommodation.* At times the defiance and noncooperation have been so strong and so skillfully targeted, and the sources of the opponents' power have been sufficiently weakened that the opponents have been left with no option but to capitulate—*nonviolent coercion.* In some rare instances, the defiance and noncooperation have been so massive, and the severance of the sources of the opponents' power had been so complete, that the regime has simply fallen apart—*disintegration.*[27]

Nonviolent social change theory suggests that there are alternative ways to pursue justice within history, ways that are more practical and more effective than violence. This is consistent with the nonviolent anti-imperial stream connected to the historical Jesus. As a Christian, I choose to follow the example of the historical Jesus, reject the preponderance of biblical material that asserts God's violent character, and pursue justice through nonviolent means. Embracing a mustard-seed vision of Christian faith leads me to reject both U.S. Empire and the various expressions of Christianity that serve that empire.[28] As a citizen, I reject U.S. Empire for practical reasons. It undermines the well-being of the republic in which I long to live and the world I care about.

Notes

1. Gene Sharp, *There Are Realistic Alternatives* (Boston: Albert Einstein Institution, 2003), 3.

2. Readers interested in the nonviolence of Jesus may find the following books helpful: Walter Wink, *Engaging the Powers: Discernment and Resistance in a World of Domination* (Minneapolis: Fortress, 1992); John Dominic Crossan, *The Birth of Christianity* (San Francisco: Harper San Francisco, 1998); Jack Nelson-Pallmeyer, *Jesus against Christianity: Reclaiming the Missing Jesus* (Harrisburg, PA: Trinity Press International, 2001); and Jack Nelson-Pallmeyer and Bret Hesla, *Worship in the Spirit of Jesus: Theology, Liturgy, and Songs without Violence* (Cleveland: Pilgrim, 2005).

3. Karen Armstrong, *Islam: A Short History* (New York: Random House, 2000), 27, 29.

4. John Dominic Crossan, *Jesus: A Revolutionary Biography* (New York: Harper Collins, 1994), 31.

5. Ibid., 39.

6. Bishop Pedro Casadaliga, *Prophets in Combat* (Oak Park, IL: Meyer Stone Books, 1987), 24–25.

7. Crossan, *Jesus: A Revolutionary Biography*, 39.

8. Richard Horsley, *Jesus and the Spiral of Violence: Popular Jewish Resistance in Roman Palestine* (Minneapolis: Fortress, 1993), 32.

9. See Nelson-Pallmeyer, *Jesus against Christianity*.

10. See Nelson-Pallmeyer and Hesla, *Worship in the Spirit of Jesus*.

11. John Dominic Crossan, *The Birth of Christianity* (San Francisco: Harper San Francisco, 1998), 391.

12. Wink, *Engaging the Powers*, 273, with emphasis in original.

13. See William R. Herzog II, *Parables as Subversive Speech: Jesus as Pedagogue of the Oppressed* (Louisville, KY: Westminster/John Knox , 1994), ch. 5.

14. Wink, *Engaging the Powers*, 182.

15. Ibid., 176, with emphasis in original.

16. Ibid.

17. Ibid., 181.

18. Robert W. Funk, Roy W. Hoover, and the Jesus Seminar, *The Five Gospels: The Search for the Authentic Words of Jesus* (New York: Scribner, 1993), 484.

19. Crossan, *Jesus: A Revolutionary Biography*, 65.

20. Thich Nhat Hanh, *Living Buddha, Living Christ* (New York: Riverhead Books, 1995), 14.

21. Ibid., 147.

22. Sharp, *There Are Realistic Alternatives*, 3.

23. Ibid.

24. Ibid., 12.

25. Ibid., 10–11.

26. Ibid., 39–48.

27. Ibid., 13–14, with emphasis in original.

28. For a book that purges Christianity of violent images of God and models worship, liturgy, and music in the nonviolent spirit of Jesus, see Nelson-Pallmeyer and Hesla, *Worship in the Spirit of Jesus.*

CHOICES

An Almighty United States, unrestrained by any rival, international body, or world opinion, bestrode the globe, a belligerent colossus determined to monopolize global oil reserves and use its vast military power to crush lesser nations or malefactors that disturbed the Pax Americana. For America's hard right—a curious farrago of Armageddon-seeking southern Protestants; neo-conservative supporters of Israel's right-wing Likud party; and the military-industrial-petroleum complex—the Bush administration's aggressive foreign policy of world domination, and utter contempt for international laws and old allies, marks a new era of national greatness. . . . But for those Americans whose primary loyalty was to their country, rather than to religious cultism, foreign nations, or financial profit, the rapid emergence of the U.S. as an imperial power waging two hugely expensive colonial wars in Asia was a disaster, both for America's democratic system and for the rest of the world.

—Eric Margolis[1]

The American rhetoric about an "evil empire," an "axis of evil," or any other earthly manifestations of the devil's handiwork is so grossly inept that one has to smile and shake one's head or else scream in outrage depending on the moment and one's personal temperament. However, it ought to be taken seriously in its decoded form. The rhetoric truthfully expresses an American obsession

with evil that is identified accusingly as emanating from outside
the country when in fact it originates from inside the United States.
The menace of evil in the United States is truly everywhere if one
thinks of the renunciation of the principle of equality, the rise of
an irresponsible plutocracy, the overdrawn credit card existence
of millions of consumers and the country as a whole, the increasing
use of the death penalty, and the return with a vengeance of obses-
sions about race. . . . God has certainly not been blessing America
lately. The country is steaming mad about the evil it sees everywhere, no doubt in part because the kettle cannot see how black it
has become.

—Emmanuel Todd[2]

Truth and Consequences

With the support of Christians the United States has been an empire for a
long time. In recent years it has moved to a rather extreme point on an
imperial continuum that has pushed beyond the economically driven
grand strategy of the Clinton years. The Bush administration has sought
global domination through permanent war, control of world oil supplies,
expansion of U.S. military bases in strategic areas throughout the world,
and military superiority, including the militarization of space. It has justified its policies with rhetoric, including references to God and divine
mission. U.S. Empire hurts people at home and throughout the world. U.S.
citizens must choose between republic and empire. Christians must also
choose, not only between republic and empire, but between violent and
nonviolent streams of Christianity.

Violent or Nonviolent Christianity?

It is problematic to challenge Jerry Falwell and Pat Robertson's explanation
that the terror attacks of 9/11 were orchestrated by a punishing God, the
politics of legalistic Christians, or George Bush's permanent war to rid
the world of evil, without formally confronting the violent theological
traditions from which they flow. The attempt to do so is emblematic of a
crisis in theology, which seems unable or unwilling to respond to the problems of U.S. Empire and accelerated religious violence traceable to many
different religious traditions worldwide.

Christian theology today, for example, is the art of choosing between incompatible and irreconcilable biblical portraits of God *without acknowledging that is what we are doing.* This sleight of hand is necessary because most Christians, whether legalistic or mainstream, are unwilling to challenge the authority of the Bible even though it is dominated by violent images of God and violent expectations of history. People who insist on holding on to the idea that violent or violence-legitimating passages in the Bible are God's word or at least inspired by God are left with two choices.

One option is to embrace the concept of God as violent, wrathful, and punishing. In this case the pathological violence associated with God in the Bible is attributed to God's actual character and does not, for example, reflect human projection. This is the view of fundamentalist, literalist, and legalistic Christians who wholeheartedly embrace God's purposeful violence as the basis and justification for U.S. Empire, including military violence in service to empire.

A second option that is common to mainstream Christians is to accommodate violent images of God without fully embracing or condemning them. Different biblical portrayals of God's character are harmonized into a theological system in which loving images somehow trump violent images of God. Accommodation allows Christians to cope with and downplay God's violence by employing a variety of strategies. At times the assumption seems to be that if something is in the Bible, it must *somehow* be true. Scriptural readings are followed with words such as "Thanks be to God" or "This is the word of the Lord" no matter how brutal the story or violent the image of God. In this way violence is legitimated even though passages containing horrific images are generally passed over quickly, read but not discussed. Other accommodating paths involve falling back onto metaphors (It's not really violence being talked about) or citing mystery (We are not God and therefore can't understand the violence and shouldn't even try).

Coping and avoidance strategies include skipping troubling verses. I call this common practice "lectionary gymnastics." Another technique is to assert, against the evidence, that God is violent in the Old Testament but loving in the New Testament. Sanitizing violence also minimizes it. Draw pictures of animals and arks and turn away from drowning humanity. Interpret Jesus' death as a sacrifice arranged by a loving God and ignore troubling questions about why a loving God needs an atoning sacrifice.

Treat the exodus as a story of liberation and turn a blind eye to divinely sanctioned genocide.

Accommodation allows Christians who may be troubled by violence to place what they most desire at the center of *their theological system,* marginalize or explain away the rest, and leave others alone to do likewise. The payoff from this approach is that it keeps challenges to scriptural authority at bay. This interest is common to many mainstream and fundamentalist Christians. The problem with this approach is that it keeps wrathful God and violent empire intact. Whether you choose to place a loving or a wrathful God (or some weird combination) at the center of *your* religious system, the wrathful God wins. This is true because although mainstream Christianity filters out some of the worst manifestations of biblical violence, the overwhelming body of biblical material is rooted in violent images of God, which other Christians embrace and use to justify violence and as the basis for Christian Empire.

Unless violent images of God and violent expectations of history are rejected specifically and forcefully, they will surface and rear their ugly heads. It is impossible, in other words, to seriously challenge dangerous expressions of Christianity that bolster violent U.S. Empire without unequivocally rejecting violent images of God that dominate the Bible. Christians living amid violent empire must, in my view, choose to take seriously the nonviolent stream associated with Jesus, not because it is more biblical or more faithful to the Gospel writers, but because it is faithful to Jesus and is a legitimate expression of Christianity. This nonviolent stream offers authentic hope in a world engulfed in violence, much of it carried out in God's name, and much of it connected to U.S. Empire.

I identified what it would mean for Christians to take the nonviolence of Jesus seriously in *Jesus against Christianity: Reclaiming the Missing Jesus.* This includes the refusal to kill other human beings or participate in any military or police force expected to use lethal violence; support for nonviolent defense efforts and international nonviolent peace and conflict resolution teams; support for multilateral institutions that work for social justice and alternatives to war and violence; support for systematic changes that seek to break the spirals of violence, including work to address the causes of hunger, poverty, indebtedness, inequality, and women's oppression; replacement of military training programs, such as ROTC, with peace studies and conflict resolution programs and centers; rejection of just-war theory; work to dramatically reduce U.S. military spending; modeling and putting nonviolent social change theory into practice; and affirming and developing the relationship between inner and outer peace.[3]

Republic or Empire?

Clyde Prestowitz in *Rogue Nation* wrote that according to the "neo-imperialists [who] believe America is exceptional," people throughout the world "will welcome the American way. . . . Thus American women and men are to be sent to the far corners of the earth on a crusade to spread the American creed to a world hungering and thirsting for it."[4] This is an idealized and misleading version of what neoconservatives and other U.S. leaders were actually seeking as they set out to implement "America's grand strategy." Prestowitz nonetheless identified five reasons why the project of the neo-imperialists would not work, reasons worth considering.

The first reason is that "there is no such thing as absolute military security." Prestowitz stated that "laser-guided bombs and nuclear missiles" don't protect us from box cutters or fanatics capable of suicide, and that "the proliferation of bases may even be increasing our risks."[5] As Chalmers Johnson, William Hartung, many others, and I have argued, U.S. military spending has almost no relationship to any legitimate defense needs of the U.S. republic.[6] In some cases it is driven by the desire to control oil supplies and other resources. In most cases, however, it serves the interests of the military-industrial complex itself and not the nation. It both bankrupts and corrupts the republic. "Lately the United States has used the notion of universal terrorism to redefine itself as the leader of a worldwide 'crusade' and to justify interventions anywhere at any time and for any length of time," Emmanuel Todd observed. "However, no historical or sociological justification of such a notion is possible for anyone willing to examine the facts of the real world."[7]

Militarized foreign policies driven by greed, fear, and the needs of a military-industrial-congressional complex undermine the well-being of citizens in the republic. President Dwight D. Eisenhower in his farewell address to the Nation, January 17, 1961, warned:

> This conjunction of an immense military establishment and a large arms industry is new in the American experience. The total influence—economic, political, even spiritual—is felt in every city, every State house, every office of the Federal government. . . . In the councils of government, we must guard against the acquisition

of unwarranted influence, whether sought or unsought, by the military industrial complex. The potential for the disastrous rise of misplaced power exists and will persist.

In 1953 Eisenhower also perceptively observed that militarism involves a monumental theft from the poor: "Every gun that is made, every warship launched, every rocket fired signifies, in the final sense, a theft from those who hunger and are not fed, those who are cold and are not clothed."[8] Not only is there no such thing as "absolute military security"; the emphasis on militarism also undermines security. Military expenditures disconnected from the legitimate defense needs of the republic rob the nation and the world of schools, teachers, houses, clean water, sanitation facilities, medical care, jobs, alternative energy technologies, environmental sustainability, and hope. U.S. military spending recently exceeded that of the rest of the world combined. In a nation and world of unmet needs, it is nothing less than obscene.

Nearly three billion people struggle to live on less than two dollars a day. A UN Human Development Report stated bluntly: "Global inequalities in income and living standards have reached grotesque proportions."[9] The "three richest people have assets that exceed the combined GDP [Gross Domestic Product] of the 48 least-developed countries." The richest 225 people have combined incomes greater than those of half of humanity. The situation is desperate but easy to improve with less greed and more political will to share the enormous bounty of the earth. Developing countries could achieve and maintain "universal access to basic education for all, basic health care for all, reproductive health care for all women, adequate food for all, and safe water and sanitation for all" at a cost of approximately forty billion additional dollars a year. "This is less than 4 percent of the combined wealth of the 225 richest people in the world"[10] and a fraction of the cost of the war with Iraq.[11]

Most U.S. citizens are not well served by empire. They are hurt by strategies for empire that undermine the republic, whether the militarized "grand strategy" of the neoconservatives or the economically driven versions of previous administrations. During the Clinton years the U.S. led the charge to corporate-led globalization that benefited elite sectors while aggravating destructive inequalities at home and abroad. Bill Moyers noted that during "the boom time of the '90s when the country achieved the longest period of economic growth in its entire history, [some] good things happened but not everyone shared equally in the benefits. To the contrary. The decade began with a sustained period of downsizing by corporations moving jobs out of America, and many of those people never recovered what was taken from them."[12]

Even before the Bush administration's vast tax giveaways to the richest Americans and the dramatic military spending increases, the United States was the most unequal of all industrial countries and the most militarized. Approximately one of five U.S. children was born into poverty. *The wealth of the richest 1 percent of U.S. households was greater than the combined total of the bottom 95 percent.* And the top 1 percent of income-earners (2.7 million people) received 50.4 percent of the national income, *more than the poorest 100 million people combined.*[13] Things deteriorated further during the Bush administration. Moyers, who called the House of Representatives "the body of Congress owned and operated by the corporate, political, and religious right,"[14] reported that over "the past three years, they've pushed through $2 trillion dollars in tax cuts—almost all tilted towards the wealthiest people in the country. Cuts in taxes on the largest incomes. Cuts in taxes on investment income. And cuts in taxes on huge inheritances. More than half of the benefits are going to the wealthiest one percent."[15] As Moyers wrote:

> Nothing seems to embarrass the political class in Washington today. Not the fact that more children are growing up in poverty in America than in any other industrial nation; not the fact that millions of workers are actually making less money today in real dollars than they did twenty years ago; not the fact that working people are putting in longer and longer hours and still falling behind; not the fact that while we have the most advanced medical care in the world, nearly 44 million Americans—eight out of ten of them in working families—are uninsured and cannot get the basic care they need. Astonishing as it seems, no one in official Washington seems embarrassed by the fact that the gap between the rich and poor is greater than it's been in 50 years—the worst inequality among all Western nations.[16]

Empires also cripple democracy. Moyers wrote that "the commonwealth" (what I call the republic) "is being upended." Politics "has become a cynical charade behind which the real business goes on—the not-so-scrupulous business of getting and keeping power in order to divide up the spoils."[17] As Donald Bartlett and James Steele have declared, we now have "government for the few at the expense of the many."[18]

A second reason the "neo-imperial" project will fail, according to Prestowitz, is because "the rest of the world doesn't necessarily see us as we see ourselves, doesn't necessarily want to *be* like us even if it likes us, and is already moving to counterbalance our power."[19] Benjamin Barber stated more forthrightly that the United States will learn a lesson that "Europeans have learned the hard way, that war never brings collective security and that preening hegemons, even when they preach peace and virtue, perhaps especially when they preach peace and virtue, are themselves likely to be the greatest peril peace faces."[20]

A third reason that ensures failure of the "neo-imperial" project, according to Prestowitz, is that "an American crusade won't work because it will increasingly involve us in the kinds of alliances of convenience and ruthless actions that only complicate our lives in the long run even as they corrupt our own character and institutions."[21] One thinks immediately of U.S. soldiers torturing Iraqi prisoners and of the deteriorating human-rights situation in many parts of the world linked to the U.S. "war on terror." Problems rooted in "alliances of convenience and ruthless actions," however, have plagued U.S. Empire for a very long time, as I have described in chapter 5.

Michael Ignatieff wrote that in many "decaying or failing states, America is hated because it is allied with regimes that have failed their people or that repress the national aspirations of the oppressed."[22] Osama bin Laden is the product of an earlier U.S. alliance with Islamic extremists. Chalmers Johnson observed a pattern of abuse common to the Soviet Union and the United States throughout the Cold War:

> Both countries wasted resources at home, undercut democracy whenever it was inconvenient abroad, promoted bloody coups and interventions against anyone who resisted their plans, and savaged the environment with poorly monitored nuclear weapons production plants. Official propagandists justified the crimes and repressions of each empire by arguing that at least a cataclysmic nuclear war had been avoided and evil intentions of the other empire thwarted or contained.[23]

A fourth reason cited by Prestowitz as to why the "neo-imperial" project will fail is that "economic globalization and American profligacy have already undermined our economic sovereignty and made us more dependent than we know on those we would dominate." The United States cannot "be the world's Caesar when we are shaking a tin cup, unless, of course we just take what we need." Prestowitz wrote:

> The charge of wanting to invade Iraq in order to control its oil, which sounds false to many American ears, has such credence abroad precisely because much of the world knows of American economic vulnerabilities and sees American military threats as intended to keep capital flowing to the American safe haven and to control the prices of vital resources so as to maintain "Bubba's" way of life. The U.S. economy is currently on an unsustainable track. Its growth is driven overwhelmingly by consumption that is based on ever-rising borrowing. As a nation, we consume increasingly more than we produce, and we are able to do so only by borrowing from abroad.[24]

The United States is a much weaker empire than the rhetoric of U.S. leaders suggests and the convictions of most U.S. citizens presume. It is, according to Emmanuel Todd, "the planet's glorious beggar" that suffers "delusions of empire." "Increasingly," Todd noted, "the rest of the world is producing so that America can consume. There is no equilibrium between exports and imports."[25] The temptation of an economically vulnerable U.S. Empire to attempt to use its otherwise useless military power to take what elite sectors want is both real and dangerous. It is another sign of the clash between empire and republic. As Todd noted, "The redevelopment of the armed forces was the result of a growing awareness of America's increasing economic vulnerability." "The security questions for a plundering country that lives off of the simple capture of outside riches are different from those that face a country that practices balanced trade in a spirit of give and take."[26] One could say, he wrote, "that America hesitated over the course of the last twenty years between two types of social and economic organization: the nation and the empire." The "imperial reshaping of American society" hit middle- and working-class Americans hard. These "imperial changes of the economy tend to transform the upper strata of American society into the upper strata of an imperial society (or 'global,' to use the current expression) that goes beyond the contours of the nation."[27]

A clear example of how the interests of U.S. citizens living in a republic are undermined by a government committed to U.S. Empire concerns energy supplies. An obvious imperial objective of the United States is to control world oil supplies. Michael Klare recognized this drive as part of a broader war for American supremacy. This war, he wrote, "will prove extremely costly in blood and treasure, and it will require ever more severe restrictions on civil liberties at home. In the final analysis, American democracy itself is put at the greatest risk by this strategy of perpetual intervention abroad."[28]

Todd described "the obsessive fixation of American foreign policy" on oil, which helps to explain U.S. support for Israel. "Obsessed by the need to control the world's oil supply, American leaders are perhaps unwilling to forego the support of the leading army in the Middle East. With its size and shape and its abundant arms, Israel sits battle ready like an enormous aircraft carrier at anchor amidst Arab seas."[29] Chalmers Johnson similarly noted that one explanation for the dramatic expansion of U.S. military bases "is the staggering level of American dependence on foreign sources of oil, which grows greater by the year. Many garrisons," he wrote, "are in foreign countries to defend oil leases from competitors or to provide police protection to oil pipelines, although they invariably claim to be doing something completely unrelated—fighting the 'war on terrorism' or the 'war on drugs,' or training foreign soldiers, or engaging in some form of 'humanitarian' intervention."[30]

Elites within an empire map the world's oil supplies and develop military policies accordingly. They stalk the world, seeking to dominate this important resource both to meet the empire's own insatiable consumption and to exercise leverage over others. Leaders of a republic, by contrast, would seek to meet the energy needs of their population by developing environmentally suitable alternatives, through conservation, and by maximizing efficiency. The republic would then seek to purchase additional needed supplies in the international market as part of "balanced trade in a spirit of give and take."

The approach of a republic has many advantages over empire and would be relatively easy to accomplish. Prestowitz pointed out, for example, that "Europe and Japan produce cars that get about 34 mpg—or ten mpg better than the U.S. fleet. If U.S. vehicles got the same fuel economy as European and Japanese vehicles, the United States would need to import no Persian Gulf oil at all." "If America had the same energy efficiency as the EU [European Union], it could not only do without oil imports from the Persian Gulf, it could [also] do without oil imports period."[31] What's more, three of the "wind-rich states—North Dakota,

Kansas, and Texas—have enough harnessable wind energy to satisfy all the nation's electricity needs."[32]

A final reason cited by Prestowitz as to why the U.S. "neo-imperial" project is doomed to fail is that "the American people don't regard body bags as symbols of their glorious valor, nor do they hanker to send their second sons or daughters into the colonial service. Having begun life in rebellion against empire," he wrote, "we never became really comfortable with the habit of empire and simply are not good imperialists."[33] We may not be good imperialists, but we are prone to fear and propaganda. This is not to deny that America's grand strategy for permanent empire will eventually crash and burn under the weight of numerous contradictions. Instead, it suggests that we are slow learners as both deficits and body bags pile up. What is abundantly clear, however, is that the ongoing implementation of the "grand strategy" would require far more numerous body bags. U.S. Empire, at least the Bush administration's version, will eventually require reinstatement of the draft. We should remember, as Benjamin Barber, warned, "The Iraq war was not a special case but part of a preventive war plan whose compass was and is the world."[34]

U.S. Empire and destructive outcomes linked to imperial ambitions did not begin and will not end with the Bush administration. They did burst into public view, however, as a result of the particular gravity of U.S. arrogance and accelerated militarization that marked U.S. foreign policy following the September 11, 2001, terrorist attacks. Thus, 9/11 provided the Bush administration with a pretext and a cover under which to implement what it called "America's grand strategy" for permanent militarized empire. The carnage left in the wake of its efforts to implement that strategy is visible both at home and abroad. It puts the need to choose between empire and republic into sharper focus.

If we are lucky and vigilant, then a good deal of hard work and soul-searching could make the most enduring legacy of neoconservative excesses something other than the destruction of Iraq, chaos in the Middle East, increased terrorism, bankruptcy of the U.S. treasury, or the deformation of religion. The high costs of U.S. Empire and the strength of the worldwide revulsion against it may lead to a long-overdue reassessment of the imperial role of the United States in the world. Rejecting empire in favor of building a healthy republic that contributes to and is part of the international community of nations is both a moral imperative and a realistic possibility.

The danger is that citizens will seek resolution to the U.S. Empire's current crisis by relying on exceptionalist rhetoric similar to what brought us here.

Myths of benevolence helped the United States become an empire many decades ago, with little public awareness or debate. These myths have built-in *exception clauses* that make it impossible to challenge either the empire or the myths themselves. There are hundreds of events that betray the myths, but each by definition is an exception, including the imperial project of the Bush administration itself. Exception clauses prevent the collective weight of all the exceptions from ever being considered, thus leaving myths and empire intact. Welcome to what novelist Gore Vidal calls "the United States of Amnesia."[35]

Those of us who are Christians living within the U.S. Empire must choose between empire and republic and between various streams of Christianity. It was perhaps inevitable that a foreign policy presenting itself as "Mother Teresa with a gun" would be backed by a "Rambo Jesus," but the problem goes deeper both politically and theologically. We must counter and transform Christian complicity with empire, including Christian theologies that ignore the radical nonviolence of Jesus and that reinforce violent images of God and violent expectations of history. Christians eager for alternative worship, liturgies, and music that reflect the non-violent spirit of Jesus can consult *Worship in the Spirit of Jesus: Theology, Liturgy, and Songs without Violence*.[36] Just as Christians need to choose between competing visions of Christianity, so too citizens must choose between competing visions of our nation: *empire or republic*. Our choices are sure to have monumental consequences for ourselves, our children, and people throughout the world.

Notes

1. Eric Margolis (contributing foreign editor), "America—the Real Danger Lies Within," *The Toronto Sun*, January 4, 2004.

2. Emmanuel Todd, *After the Empire: The Breakdown of the American Order* (New York: Columbia University Press, 2002), 120.

3. Jack Nelson-Pallmeyer, *Jesus against Christianity: Reclaiming the Missing Jesus* (Harrisburg, PA: Trinity Press International, 2001), 347–49.

4. Clyde Prestowitz, *Rogue Nation: American Unilateralism and the Failure of Good Intentions* (New York: Basic Books, 2003), 274–75.

5. Ibid., 275.

6. See Chalmers Johnson, *The Sorrows of Empire: Militarism, Secrecy, and the End of the Republic* (New York: Metropolitan Books, 2004); and William Hartung, *How Much Are You Making on the War, Daddy?* (New York: Nation Books, 2003).

7. Todd, *After the Empire*, 44.

8. Similar sentiments are expressed within a variety of religious traditions, including Catholic social teaching. For example the pope's encyclical *Gaudium et spes* (*The Pastoral Constitution on the Church in the Modern World*), ratified on December 7, 1965, says: "The arms race is one of the greatest curses on the human race and the harm it inflicts on the poor is more than can be endured" (par. 81).

9. Quoted by Paul Street, "Free to Be Poor," *Z Magazine*, June 2001, 25.

10. Chuck Collins et al., *Shifting Fortunes: The Perils of the Growing American Wealth Gap* (Boston: United for a Fair Economy, 1999), 18.

11. See "The War in Iraq Cost the United States . . . [and Counting]," www.costofwar.com/.

12. Bill Moyers, "The Fight of Our Lives," *Alternet*, posted on June 16, 2004, printed on June 24, 2004, 2, www.alternet.org/story/18954/.

13. Chuck Collins and Felice Yeskel, *Economic Apartheid in America* (New York: New Press, 2000), 39, with emphasis added.

14. Moyers, "Fight of Our Lives," 2.

15. Ibid., 5.

16. Ibid.

17. Ibid., 4.

18. Quoted by Moyers, "Fight of Our Lives," 5.

19. Prestowitz, *Rogue Nation*, 275, with emphasis in original.

20. Benjamin R. Barber, *Fear's Empire: War, Terrorism, and Democracy* (New York: W. W. Norton, 2003), 56.

21. Ibid., 276.

22. Michael Ignatieff, *Empire Lite: Nation-building in Bosnia, Kosovo and Afghanistan* (London: Vintage, 2003), 9.

23. Johnson, *Sorrows of Empire*, 32–33.

24. Prestowitz, *Rogue Nation*, 276.

25. Todd, *After the Empire*, xxi, 63.

26. Ibid., 85.

27. Ibid., 71–72.

28. Michael Klare, "Resources," in *Power Trip: U.S. Unilateralism and Global Strategy after September 11* (ed. John Feffer; New York: Seven Stories, 2003), 60.

29. Ibid., 87, 114.

30. Johnson, *Sorrows of Empire*, 167.

31. Prestowitz, *Rogue Nation*, 82–83.

32. *Sierra Magazine*, July/August 2002, 30; cf. Lester R. Brown, "Europe Leads the Way to Wind Energy Age," *Peopleandplanet.net*, www.peopleandplanet.net/doc.php?id=2198.

33. Prestowitz, *Rogue Nation*, 276.

34. Barber, *Fear's Empire*, 41.

35. Gore Vidal, *Perpetual War for Perpetual Peace: How We Got to Be So Hated* (New York: Thunder's Mouth/Nation's Books, 2002), ix.

36. Jack Nelson-Pallmeyer and Bret Hesla, *Worship in the Spirit of Jesus: Theology, Liturgy, and Songs without Violence* (Cleveland: Pilgrim, 2005).

EPILOGUE

The "grand strategy" implemented during President Bush's first four years in office was aimed at establishing permanent U.S. global supremacy through the unilateral use of military power. Its recklessness and the carnage left in its wake brought the problem of empire into sharper focus. The politics of lies, deception, and fear on which it was based led many people outside our borders to see the United States as the gravest threat to the world since the rise of Nazi Germany. Many people outside the United States viewed the election between Bush and Kerry as a referendum between a known insanity and the *possibility* of something different. The election would measure just how sick the U.S. body politic had become which in turn would reveal how dangerous the United States was likely to be in the years to come.

Most frightening to many, and what led to comparisons with pre-Nazi Germany, was the fact that there was *any chance* that those responsible for so many destructive policies *could be reelected*. Hitler, it should be remembered, had a popular mandate too. Pre-Nazi Germany comparisons were also drawn in light of Christian support for the disastrous policies of the Bush administration. The election, therefore, was seen as a referendum on religion. It would measure the depth and breadth of intolerant, theocratic, Taliban-like Christianity that fostered hatred of others and made the almost unimaginable prospect of reelecting George W. Bush a real and dangerous possibility.

The election of John Kerry would not have miraculously ended the many problems associated with U.S. Empire. For much of the world, however, a Bush defeat would have meant that the majority of the U.S. electorate had repudiated the neoconservatives, recognized and responded to their nation's imperial folly and to the dangerous ascendancy of reactionary militarism and equally reactionary religion. A Kerry victory meant that there was at least the possibility that the United States would relate to the world in different ways.

A significant part of the U.S. electorate also viewed the election as a referendum between madness and possibility. Madness claimed victory but the determination and strength of those who long for and are willing to work for alternatives offer impressive signs of hope. The 2004 electoral process and outcome, however, confirm many of my deepest concerns.

First, the politics of fear dominated the election. Nearly every political advertisement for President Bush and other republican candidates were specifically designed to create and capitalize on fear. Goering's words quoted previously about how easy it is for leaders to muster support for war and other disastrous policies are haunting: "All you have to do is tell them they are being attacked, and denounce the peacemakers for lack of patriotism and exposing the country to danger. It works the same in any country." Kerry bought into the rhetoric of a dangerous world in which others are out to get us and he cast himself as the one more capable to lead the nation amidst such dangers.

The politics of fear was so pervasive and so successful that concerns about terrorism and security led many people to vote for President Bush who was arguably guilty of state-sponsored terrorism. President Bush did little to protect the homeland before or after 9-11, generated unprecedented hatred of the United States, used 9-11 as cover to pursue policies he knew would result in increased threats of terror, invaded and left Afghanistan and especially Iraq in chaos, and reenergized al-Qaeda. That people voted for Bush *because* they were concerned about terrorism brought to mind a quote from Adolf Hitler, "What good fortune for those in power that the people do not think."

Second, neither Bush nor Kerry seriously challenged the problems of empire or contemplated the profound choices we must make between empire and republic. The United States is a declining empire. Bush invaded Iraq as part of a "grand strategy" for global domination. Kerry never acknowledged our illegal occupation of Iraq and the best he could offer was a "solution" based on more troops. Bush and Kerry agreed on maintaining our disastrous support for Israel at the expense of Palestinians, on maintaining or increasing the imperial military budget of the United States, and the U.S. militarization of space has bipartisan support.

A second Bush term could be disastrous for the nation and the world. The United States is a nation with enormous destructive capacity but with little useable military power. It is a nation whose economic weakness will become more and more pronounced in the years to come. If the United States were to transition from empire to republic gracefully this would benefit its citizens and the world. If U.S. elites seek to defend and expand empire then they will wreak havoc both domestically and internationally. The "great revulsion" within the United States didn't reach fruition in this election but it will come. The decision for republic over empire will be imposed by a visionary, outraged, and organized populace that has much work to do in reshaping the imperial assumptions of the nation's leaders.

Third, the electoral campaign and outcome demonstrate the extreme militarization of our culture, our minds, our media, our politicians, our faith traditions, and our lives. Both candidates and many of their supporters embraced the idea that superior violence saves. In many ways, Kerry sought to win the election by out-militarizing Bush. He would hunt down and kill the terrorists more effectively. He would send more troops to do the job right and spend whatever it takes to equip our soldiers. Militarism is a serious disease attacking and destroying healthy cells in the body politic.

Fourth, the outcome of the election confirms how dangerously far the United States has moved in the direction of theocracy. Arguably one of the most immoral administrations in the nation's history received support from Christians concerned about "morality." Ecocide, war, torture, lies, deceit, dramatic increases in the number of abortions worldwide, concentrating wealth in the hands of elites, crony capitalism, encouraging hatred of gays, and saddling future generations with unimaginable debt did not factor into the moral equation for theocratic Christians who supported Bush. The House, the Senate, the White House, and the Supreme Court (with new appointments coming) are all controlled by a Republican party that has been taken over by legalistic, fundamentalist, Armageddon expecting Christians. The crisis of theocracy also includes the fact that significant segments of Protestant Christianity remain captive to nationalism, war, and patriotism, and, that many Catholics embrace exclusionary and reactionary politics based on concern about gay marriage and abortion. The republic, through a combination of these religious forces, is under serious attack.

The choices before us are clear. As citizens we must choose republic over empire and as Christians we need to embrace "mustard seed" varieties of Christian faith while working to challenge imperial, theocratic Christianities that threaten the republic. I close with words of hope, words about hope, from Barbara Kingsolver's novel, *Animal Dreams* in which Hallie is writing from Nicaragua to her sister Codi in the United States:

Wars and elections are both too big and too small to matter in the long run. The daily work—that goes on, it adds up. It goes into the ground, into crops, into children's bellies and their bright eyes. Good things don't get lost. Codi, here's what I've decided: the very least you can do in your life is to figure out what you hope for. And the most you can do is live inside that hope. . . . What I want is so simple I almost can't say it: elementary kindness. Enough to eat, enough to go around. The possibility that kids might one day grow up to be neither the destroyers nor the destroyed. . . . Right now I'm living in that hope. . . .[1]

Notes

1. The quote is from Barbara Kingsolver, *Animal Dreams*, (New York: Harper Collins, 1990), 299.

INDEX